PRAISE FOR

Both staff and clients commented that this was a great way to get a message across without feeling as if you were being lectured to. They laughed and learned–and some even cried–but most importantly, they came away with a new awareness of some of the very issues they have faced in their lives. — *Donna Murphy, Greater Portland YWCA*

It made me reflect on myself, and think that maybe my relationship isn't as great as I thought it was, and I should do something about it. — *Anon. Student*

The Marines at Marine Corps Air Station Iwakuni were very impressed with the performance. We would love to bring *You the Man* back to Iwakuni for our High School students. Lloyd Watts did an amazing job. Everyone at the Air Station is raving about his performance. Thank you so much for sharing your program with us. — *Shermona Hart, Victim Advocate, Marine Corps Air Station Iwakuni, Japan*

Getting young people to talk about healthy and unhealthy relationships, violence in relationships, and sexual assault is not an easy task. The beauty of *You The Man* is that it stimulates conversations without creating blame and controversy between the sexes…. It was impossible for students to avoid relating to at least one of the characters of the show. The production encouraged conversations about the points at which a relationship might become unhealthy, what to do, how to help. We didn't have to spend a lot of time arguing over whose fault "it" was, a typical reaction occurring in similar discussions with sophomores in high school. The conversations are continuing two weeks after the show. — *Nancy Gaynor, Counselor, and Nancy Bird, Director of Health Services, The Hotchkiss School*

I appreciate the fact that the program was entertaining while still realistically portraying the issues surrounding domestic and sexual violence. I like the fact that the audience did not need to infer much information from the play — the characters talk openly to the viewer about warning signs, concerns, safety planning, and what they can do about the situation. The play represents tangible options for everyone involved... I am a strong believer in the fact that the issues surrounding domestic and sexual violence are not simply women's issues, and utilizing the male voice in your play seems to be very effective. Combining that with the bystander approach, everyone can relate to the characters, showing the males in the audience that they can play a role in stopping, and ultimately preventing, violence against women. — *Jennifer Turco, AmeriCorps Victim Assistance Program Advocate placed at Rape and Assault Support Services, Inc.*

FABULOUS! We had almost a full house. [The actor] received a STANDING OVATION! Just so you know that is no easy feat from students... The students really connected with him. — *Kelly Horner, Director, Sexual Assault Resource Center SUNY Albany*

The program went really well! I just got back to my office and can breathe a sigh of relief. Lloyd did a great job and you can tell from the kids' faces that they were all totally captivated by the performance. I'm just now looking at the filled-out evaluation forms and at first glance I see that the students all thought the show was "excellent", "amazing", "very interesting", "very well done", and "well acted." — *Ellen Birnbaum, Legislative Aide to Councilwoman Lee Seeman, Town of North Hempstead, Manhasset, NY*

Although the topic of *You the Man* can be uncomfortable for many, I am glad Hermon High School took the risk to bring the play to our students, faculty, and staff. If the play made a positive impact on just one person, it was worth the time and effort. I know from the evaluations and from talking to students that lives were changed for the better as some took the message very personally realizing that a change in their behavior was necessary. It was extremely healing for others. —*Shelley Gavett, Teacher, Hermon High School, Hermon, ME*

As a psychologist and coordinator for women's programming, I am always searching for unique ways to educate undergraduates about violence against women. Although the literature in this area is encouraging prevention programming to be tailored towards men, it is often difficult to find such resources. *You the Man* is one of the few programs that engage men as full partners in the fight to end violence against women. I believe presenting the information about violence against women in a theatrical format was particularly effective because it bypassed the typical resistance students erect when attending a program of this kind. —*Courtney Aberle, PhD., Coordinator of the Women's Center, Southern Methodist University, Dallas, TX*

We are still so appreciate of Eddie's performance this year! We gave a report to the Board of Trustees in the beginning of May of the work we are doing in our Human Development Curriculum, which sponsored *You the Man*. We invited four students to serve on a panel that gave information to the Board. Two of the students cited the performance as one of the most memorable experiences of the year. I have passed this on to our director of Counseling. Again, many thanks for your support in bringing *You the Man* to Millbrook. —*Cam Hardy, Millbrook Academy*

The performance was interactive, engaging, and creative. —*France Keene, Virginia Tech Victim Services Adjudication Coordinator*

This was a wonderfully and skillfully done play. Very thought provoking; Guy is truly great at drawing in the audience and Cathy's scripting was brilliant. We were lucky to have this come to our community. —*Anon., Eastern Maine Task Force on Domestic Violence quarterly meeting, Bangor, ME*

I'm sure you've heard this a zillion times but this is an incredible performance. I don't think there is any area of relationship abuse you don't touch on. I wish every college and high school male and female student could see this. —*Pat Jenkins, audience member, Bangor, ME*

I can't think of a better way to reach our youth regarding such a serious issue. —*Amanda Cost, School-Based Advocate, Spruce Run Domestic Violence Project, Bangor, ME*

OTHER BOOKS BY ADD VERB PUBLICATIONS

Out & Allied: An Anthology of Performance Pieces Written by LGBTQ Youth & Allies, Vol. 1 (Maine Writers & Publishers Alliance Award, Best Anthology 2012)

Out & Allied: An Anthology of Performance Pieces Written by LGBTQ Youth & Allies, Vol. 2

The Thin Line: A Play About Ending the Silence on Eating Disorders

When Turtles Make Love: A Play on Parents and Teens and the Big Talk

Money Talks: Theatre for Financial Literacy

A Play and Program on Bystanders, Sexual Assault & Dating Violence

FIRST EDITION

Add Verb Publications

A Play and Program on Bystanders, Sexual Assault & Dating Violence

FIRST EDITION

© 2018, Cathy Plourde
All rights reserved

The contributors of this book may have changed names and other identifying elements of their narratives to protect privacy. *You the Man* is a work of fiction. The characters are a product of the playwright's imagination and any resemblance to real people is entirely coincidental. The materials in this book are for documentary purposes only and individuals and organizations are responsible for seeking their own professional guidance in any performance or educational program that would address sexual violence.

No part of this book may be used or reproduced in any manner whatsoever without written permission except in the case of brief quotations embodied in critical articles and reviews. For information contact: addverblicensing@gmail.com.

The scanning, uploading, and distribution of this book via the Internet or via any other means without the permission of the publisher is illegal and punishable by law. Please purchase only authorized editions, and do not participate or encourage piracy of copyrighted materials. Your support of the authors' rights is appreciated.

Printed in the USA
Interior and cover design by K. Larson
Cover image design by Zach Magoon

LCCN: 2017939475
ISBN-10: 099135284X
ISBN-13: 978-0-9913528-4-5

Add Verb Publications

Books in Add Verb Publications catalogue may be purchased for educational, business, or sales promotional use.
For information please write: addverblicensing@gmail.com

To Sue Bradford and Noel Tewes. Thank you for opening your door and for all of the oatmeal sessions.

LICENSING INFORMATION

You the Man is copyright protected and all rights are reserved and are held by the author. No duplication or production without permission.

To request amateur or professional rights for performing *You the Man* write to: addverblicensing@gmail.com (Note that there are two Ds!)

If you are planning a reading for a group, conference, or an awareness week event, please send a note to the email above as we would like to be able to share how *You the Man* is being used around the world.

CONTENTS

Playwright's Note 11

Actors on Performing *You the Man* 19

You the Man (Annotated US Script) 27

Actor Prop & Travel Checklist 64

Site Coordinator Checklist 66

Production Guide 68

You the Man in Cultural Translation (by Ann Taket, Prod.) 86

You the Man (Australian Script) 91

10 You The Man

PLAYWRIGHT'S NOTE

A few years prior to drafting *You the Man* in 2001, I wrote the *The Thin Line,* a one-woman, multi-character performance on coping with eating disorders. At its first staged reading a friend of the teenage actor I had found to perform said, in evident frustration, "Yes, we know that our friends have this problem. What we don't know is what to do about it." She cut to the quick with her remark. It is not enough to raise awareness or illustrate the truth about complex, critical issues; nor is it useful to lob over-simplified solutions at them. I took her point to heart and used this idea of "So what?" as a litmus test for the educational theatre that I created afterwards, which greatly influenced how I approached *You the Man*.

Outside of research on the subject itself, the other influences on craft came from a combination of Augusto Boal's work in using performance as a rehearsal for change, a feminist perspective on multiplicity of perspectives (not either/or, right/wrong), and Louis E. Catron's book *The Power of One: The Solo Play for Playwrights, Actors, and Directors.* A list of factors led me to decide on a short, scripted, multi-character production to be professionally performed:

- Improv-based theatre can often be used to great effect in educational settings; however, I did not want to leave key points to chance in the improv process.

- I did not want a lack of actor training or talent—artistic merit—to open these sensitive issues to public ridicule.

- I also had a sense of the optimal length of the play for the school assembly setting, which would still privilege time for the audience to ask questions of the advocates.

- And, having seen theatre on this topic that I found agonizing, antagonizing, or otherwise objectionable (e.g., victim-blaming, an over-simplification of the issues, or emotionally jarring), I knew I wanted to do something different.

You the Man is entirely fictional but came out of research, my experience working with domestic violence and sexual violence (DV/SA) advocates, and conversations with people around the United States who were at the forefront of the work to engage men in violence prevention and intervention. A conversation with an advocate crystalized the idea that the script would feature male voices: she said she was repeatedly frustrated during school presentations because she could see that the boys tuned her out. Script development included listening, gathering, and considering context. Many people had been doing work in DV/SA for a long time, and I knew they knew more than I did about best practices. They could tell me where they struggled to deliver messages, what was helpful, where the field was headed, and even what they would do if equipped with a magic wand.

As I sorted through the different aspects of DV/SA teaching points, myths, and challenges, I had a list of objectives:

- To make the approach be far away from "shock-u-drama."

- To honor the fact of victims and survivors being present in every room, at every performance.

- To recognize the equal potential of perpetrators also being in the room.

- To be respectful of the fact that the audiences are often captive/non-volunteering audiences (as is the norm with school assemblies).

- To make sure the script, acting, and direction did not re-traumatize survivors, did not glamorize violence, and was rich with accurate information.

- To provide content that allows for triangulation—meaning that we can talk about what happened in the play instead of what happened at a party last week, especially if that is what happened at the party or is similar to what you, your friends, or a family member have experienced.

- To leave a community stronger than before, aware of and engaged with their local resources, equipped with knowledge of what DV/SA looks like, and an increased sense of responsibility, as well as tools to do something when they see it happening around them.

The play was envisioned as a tool for agencies and advocates, a means of conveying facts and information in a palatable package in order to leave the advocates free to engage in real dialogue with their audiences. Since *You the Man* was launched, many other programs have come into being—some even created by people who were inspired by this play—and yet the topic has only moved from "cutting edge" to "more and more relevant" every day.

The play began touring in 2002 under the company name Add Verb Productions Arts & Education, and was first performed by Guy Durichek. Guy stuck with it throughout the development process and regular re-writes. With every season, tweaks and adjustments were made to the script to both stay current and to maximize the opportunity to present a world in which men and boys are key to societal change and are acknowledged as potential victims and survivors themselves.

It was more difficult to find the right actors for *You the Man* than it was for *The Thin Line* (which has four characters), as this new show had six characters of a wider range of ages and types.

These characters require a virtuoso actor to nuance and reflect their emotional journey and growth and not get mired in stereotypes. And, the topic is highly charged: statistics from the US Department of Justice, which are helpfully distilled on the websites of the Rape, Abuse, and Incest National Network, National Children's Advocacy Center, and Futures Without Violence (or any of the many other national and regional organizations dedicated to addressing violence), point out that men and women have nearly the same rate of victimization, whether or not data is being collected or reported.

One other difference between *You the Man* and *The Thin Line* has had to do with actor participation on the panel. With *You the Man*, the actors were often the only male on the panel, and so, between the bond they had with the audience and by the mere virtue of being male, they could have easily dominated the conversation. However, the actors were coached to turn the questions requiring advocacy expertise to the other panelists. Having trained as actors and not as advocates, this was most appropriate, and gave the added benefit of modeling making room for women's voices.

You the Man has been performed for audiences of a range ages without any changes to the script. The biggest difference with the program has been in the post show discussions, which are tailored to suit the audience. With a few exceptions in the US, it was primarily presented to high schools, colleges, and at conferences and trainings for those who do work with youth. The actor's race—Caucasian, Latino, African-American, and in Australia, of Aboriginal descent—was not neutral, and it could be a barrier or an advantage depending on the circumstances, demographics, and social climate within the community for which they were performing. Due to the rigorous process of preparing the community to have the production come in, appropriately, the play didn't go anywhere were the leadership was not willing, and we never pursued audiences such as juvenile detention centers where we felt it would ultimately be unsafe for audiences. Interestingly, where *You the Man* frequently returned to the same school year after year, the site coordinators often bonded with their *You the Man*-man, and didn't like it when a different one had to be sent due to hiring changes or actor availability!

At times high school youth and university-aged young adults alike could be hostile, especially if attendance was required for something they were sure was going to be a waste of their time. These audiences are especially intolerant of bad theatre and they are not interested in being polite if they feel bored, condescended to, or otherwise put off. Every actor learned that they had to win their audience over in the first ten seconds or it was going to be a long and uncomfortable show; this was perhaps even more so for *You the Man* than *The Thin Line*. This do-or-die challenge forced the actors to dig deep in their box of tricks—I highly recommend Keith Jonstone's book I*mpro: Improvisation and the Theater*—to keep the stakes high and to be true. It helped, according to the actors, to hold the thought that every audience included victims and survivors.

Direct address-style performance is quite different from a play that has people talking to each other on the stage. Direct address is exciting and frightening: there is nowhere to hide. The connection that the actor has with the audience—which he or she must establish for *each* character—is supported and made even more intense by Add Verb's policy to leave the house lights as well as the stage lights up for the whole performance and post-show discussion. More often than not, these two plays have been done in non-theatre venues, with a negligible separation between the playing area and the audience. Sometimes the actors were faced with people scowling at them from the front row or talking or texting in the back row. Body language would reveal deep discomfort or deep attention. When we've been able to track down why a small group of people wouldn't stop talking throughout the show it was usually because they were connecting the events of the play with a person in a situation closely related. Even though these audience members were completely engaged, this kind of behavior was hard on the actor. Reading and respectfully riding the emotional energy of the audience, and knowing the script well enough to use it to shift audiences in a different direction was a skill the actors learned on their feet.

16 You The Man

The stories of how *You the Man* has impacted people's lives are incredibly moving. What hits me the hardest is the number of times I've been told that someone had seen the show months or even years prior, and then one day found themselves in circumstances in which they realized they needed help, citing the play as a part of the recognition process.

During the talk-back after the very first showing of the play, which happened to be at a private school in Connecticut, I listened and grew goose bumps: the students were quoting the language of the play verbatim in their discussion. It seemed as though they had sponged up the words and plot lines and were eagerly using it to talk about relationships, sexuality, and fears.

A lot of theatre is delivered under the headings of "social change," "wellness," or "education." However, measuring the impact of this kind of theatre is extraordinarily difficult and most evidence of educational theatre's efficacy is from surveys collected immediately following performances. Unfortunately, this is only taking in an emotional response rather than a measure of attitude or behavior change. Testimonials from administrators and professionals helped inspire confidence in Add Verb's programs, and more than one new booking came because a sister school had brought it in and spoke well of the experience. We felt confidant that it was working, but we had no quanitifialbe data.

With funding from The Bingham Program, a charitable endowment at Tufts Medical Center, I worked with a team of researchers at the University of New England to design and implement an Institutional Review Board-approved longitudinal study for both *The Thin Line* and *You the Man*. An article entitled *You the Man: theatre as bystander education in dating violence presented findings in the peer-reviewed publication,* (*The Journal of Arts & Health*, October 2015) gives the details, but the study supports what we had believed and seen anecdotally over the years: that students increased their knowledge and were more likely to intervene on behalf of someone they knew who was experiencing violence, and that much of this knowledge and likelihood of behavior was sustained over time. Many audience members reported attempting an intervention on someone's behalf. A similar study on *You the Man* has been undertaken by Professor Ann Taket at Deakin University in Melbourne, Australia, and is in the publishing process, reporting positive early indicators.

Between 2002 and 2014 *You the Man* toured as an Add Verb production, and its success credits the work of a number of booking agents, interns, and administrators, but mostly it was due to the actors who traveled solo, equipped with only their talent and a bag of props: Guy Durichek, Eddie Martinez, Walter (Tre) Simpson III, Tim Collins (a solo performer who continues to base some of his work on his experience with *You the Man*), Lloyd Watts, Dan Haggerty, Keith Anctil, and Brian Chamberlain (in roughly chronological order). In Australia, John Shearman, Glenn Maynard, and Chris Asimos have performed a cultural translation of *You the Man*, directed by the renowned opera and theatre director, Suzanne Chaundy, and produced by Prof. Ann Taket (Deakin University, Melbourne, Victoria), who led the Australian writing team (Ann, myself, Virginia Murray, and Patrick Van Der Werf).

To all of these actors, booking agents, administrative and creative teams; board members, donors, and foundations; and individuals, students, and families who convinced their schools and communities to book the program: Thank You! And to the dedicated, passionate site coordinators in each community who (usually outside of their job description) made the production possible: Thank you. You have let literally thousands upon thousands of people know that they are not alone. There is help when they are ready to leave an abusive relationship. There are experts who can work with them in the aftermath of sexual trauma. And, as bystanders, there are alternatives to silence.

18 You The Man

ACTORS ON PERFORMING *YOU THE MAN*

Over the years the actors who performed You the Man *had many tales to tell of what happened during performances and in the ensuing conversations. Several of them have volunteered reflections on what it was like to perform the play and what they would share with others considering a production. ~CP*

BRIAN: As actors we often take on projects that we feel will be challenging or a lot of fun, or frankly, we just have an irrational need to act. Sometimes I end the show feeling like I did a good job at entertaining, or that perhaps I stretched myself, or sometimes I leave not having had the best of experiences. Whatever the case may be, I have always left a show knowing that I have actually helped someone. *You The Man* gave me this gift and it has forever changed how I approach any new role, and also how I engage life. This show will bend you…if you allow it to.

Brian Chamberlain
Shelburne, New Hampshire

20 You The Man

GLENN: Being involved in this project is both a blessing and a curse, especially as an actor. In the half hour performance and subsequent panel discussion that follows, my heart feels like it is constantly breaking as I am confronted by the grotesque realities of the issues raised in the script and the ensuing discussion. It is uplifting to hear professionals in their respective fields talk with such passion and enthusiasm, and it is both inspiring and devastating beyond words to hear the stories of survivors when they are brought up in these discussions.

The more times I perform *You The Man*, the more my head fills with the statistics and stories of domestic violence and sexual assault in my country; the more sickened I feel, the more resolute I become to do what I can to improve this situation in any way and by every means available to me. This show does change attitudes. It does equip people with the tools to assist themselves or others in the event of, or the prevention of, an incident.

I truly appreciate the importance and magnitude of this work and I employ every tool I have in my little box of 'Acting Tricks'. My role is to tell the story, to lead the audience through the awful events that are raised in the show — to give them a real sense of the damage to and grief felt by the victims and their families, friends, acquaintances, and colleagues. To deliver to them the teaching points so they may walk away with the tools to become empowered enough to speak up or reach out as required. And to do so in a way that does not leave the audience completely shattered.

There is a fine line that I walk, as an actor, to allow myself to feel everything, while not becoming distracted or completely overwhelmed by these emotions. I was fortunate to work with director Suzanne Chaundy, and every rehearsal felt like an acting lesson. I am a better actor and performer for working with her.

I am a good man. I have enormous respect for all the women in my life. But, that's not enough. I am indebted to Cathy Plourde, Suzanne Chaundy, and producer Ann Tacket for including me in this project and giving me the opportunity to make a difference, to bring change in others or assist in the creation of safer places for women and girls… for everyone!

> Glenn Maynard
> Melbourne, Australia

EDDIE: When I auditioned for *You the Man* I initially wanted to do it because I knew it would be something very challenging as an actor. Playing six different characters on stage all by myself is no easy feat. Soon after we began rehearsing, I realized it was much bigger than just acting. In just a few weeks, I learned so much about domestic abuse it was overwhelming: the unbelievable statistics; the different types of abuse (not just physical); how often women get re-victimized by society; and, the importance of not just standing by but doing something about it.

The show is unique in the way that it is presented — coming from the male's perspective, and not just one male but the different male archetypes that would encounter these issues. Looking back now, as a husband and father, I understand the importance of teaching young girls to let their light shine through. To make their voices be heard and to make them feel that they are not alone. But I think the biggest lesson is that it is not enough just to teach my little girls all of this but I must teach my son as well, probably even more so. That is why I believe this show is crucial for young adults to experience. It's presented in a way they can relate to and without being preachy, it gives young men and women the options they have if ever faced with these kinds of situations.

One of the things that I personally took from doing the show all of those years is that as a man, it is not only about not being an abuser, but also about your obligation to speak up and not tolerate those who are.

> Eddie Martinez
> Los Angeles, California

JOHN: *You The Man* is a real challenge for the performer. Multiple characters, high levels of technical skill, ever-changing performance spaces and, more than any play I've ever done before, it requires oodles of courage.

Audiences for *You The Man* are not always receptive to hearing what this play has to say. They're not your usual theatregoers — some have never even seen a play and suddenly find themselves forced into watching one. The most hostile audiences I've ever faced as an actor have been in service of this play and its important message, such as: Regional Football players who are annoyed their training was cancelled to sit through you monologuing for half an hour; or a school where the students spend their time trying to intimidate and derail the performance before it even starts. I could go on — but the more important thing is that these were also by far the most rewarding experiences. You'll see for yourself, this play works. Trust the text and it hits its target dead-on. These audiences see right through you if you're being false or playing fast and loose with the truth. They force you to rise to the occasion. As a result, those audiences were more often than not the ones where the discussion would have raged for hours if not for the time limit imposed by the moderator. They were the audiences who personally came to thank you, or stopped you on the street the next day to chat about the content.

As actors, we really should be seeing ourselves as agents for cultural change, but the sad reality is that nowadays a lot of our work is purely for commercial gain. This work made me proud to call myself an actor and to Cathy, Suzanne, and Anne I am tremendously grateful.

> *John Shearman*
> *Melbourne, Australia*

GUY: In late summer of 2001, I had the great fortune to meet Cathy Plourde on the set of a small indie film we were both cast in. Cathy was looking for an actor to help her workshop a new play and had received an endorsement on my behalf. After the staged reading, Cathy took a leap of faith and hired me as the first actor for this piece even though she initially felt she wanted a younger actor. Weeks of rehearsals, conversations, and countless hours of memorization later, *You The Man* had its Maine premiere in a beautiful space in Portland, complete with local television and newspaper crews handy. *The Portland Press Herald* ran a feature article in the lifestyle section of their paper—the cover photo was of Cathy and myself, looking VERY serious.

I have never had a finer moment in my career as an actor. I keep a framed copy of that photo on my wall.

Over the course of the next two years, I performed *You The Man* in over 80 different venues for thousands of audience members including public and private high schools, colleges and universities, and for health care and education professionals. Every place I traveled to was in need of the message, some desperately as they struggled with situations mirrored in the story line of the play. Schools where a star athlete had been accused by a fellow student of date rape. Private post-secondary academies where the student body had a reputation for heckling a presenters off-stage. The bookings started slowly, but as more and more people witnessed the show, the bookings became steadier. I am so very proud to have been there at the inception of *You The Man*, and without hesitation, call it the most important piece of theater I have ever had the privilege of working on.

For my fellow actors cast in this piece, I give what little wisdom I have. I was fortunate enough to have already been years into the process of re-defining for myself what "healthy masculinity" looked and felt like. This on-going journey included private therapy as well as finding other men who were like-minded and willing to work with each other to create new ways of being. In short, DO YOUR OWN WORK! Yes, we are actors, but more importantly we are sons, brothers, and, some of us, fathers. We live in a world where staying silent is essentially giving the green light to our brothers we see engaged in abusive/unhealthy behavior. Be prepared to "own up" to your own behavior, however minuscule it may seem, and to face your preconceived bias of any given audience. There is no fourth wall here. You will see and hear tears midway through a performance that will break your heart; you will feel audience members shrivel and wilt as some character's words ring true; you will become angry at the giggles and guffaws from others. Try to stay centered every time. Find the TRUTH of each character in whatever way you can: there is no phoning in performances on this one! What a rare and beautiful gift it is that we are the standard-bearers of this message. And let the professionals BE the professionals! I made the mistake early on of trying to answer questions during Q&A forums that I had no business answering. We can talk about the intricacies of creating characters, the nuances of scene shifts, but at the end of the day, let the pros deal with the nuts and bolts of how and where to find help, numbers to call, and what services are available.

Finally, I am proud to call you a fellow 'Man'… there are just a handful of us, and even though I don't know you, you are a brother to me now in that we have had a chance to speak the same words… your work WILL make a difference!

Guy Durichek
New Hampshire

A solo performance addressing bystanders, dating abuse, and sexual violence.

By Cathy Plourde

You the Man
by Cathy Plourde

Copyright © CATHY PLOURDE. 2000, 2002, 2009, 2015, 2018.

DO NOT DUPLICATE OR DISTRIBUTE OR PERFORM
WITHOUT PERMISSION FROM PLAYWRIGHT
License inquiries to: addverblicensing@gmail.com

A solo performance addressing bystanders, dating abuse, and sexual violence.

By Cathy Plourde

ANNOTATED SCRIPT AND PRODUCTION NOTES

Characters

STAN THE MAN: A merchant of cool with a message.

VIRGIN LARRY: Athlete bumping against the walls of the macho box.

MITCHELL: Bystander compelled to act as he realizes his friend, Jana, is in increasing danger.

MICHAEL: Jana's dad, not currently living with her. Not a great communicator, he struggles to stay connected to his daughter.

OFFICER FRIENDLY: Has a sense of humor and a knack for disarming young adults who don't really want to hear about sexual violence.

DR. WING: Jana's teacher. Orchestrates an intervention safely and with care.

Staging

The actor's use of space helps to define each character as he is being played. The playing area is roughly a wide flattened triangle or V shape, with the apex USC and the wide part of the triangle/V along front of the stage. Depth of the playing area shouldn't be more than 3 paces and the width is ideally 5 or 6 paces. Expand or contract as required, but keep the playing area tight for consistency in crossing and timing.

Lighting

Whether a lighting design for the stage is used or not, the house lights are left on, though may be dimmed somewhat during the performance. The intention is that the audience can still see each other and the actor can see the audience.

Costume and Props

A neutral black outfit such as jeans, a T-shirt or button-up without branding, and rubber soled black boots or shoes that don't draw attention. (No clogs, squeaky shoes, or anything flashy or reflective.) Athletic pants are possible but can look too casual to too trendy.

Use props and accessories to signal characters: sunglasses (Stan the Man); snack (Mitchell); ball cap and basketball (Virgin Larry); cell phone (Michael); and, lab coat and glasses (Dr. Wing).

Preset:

- Table, 4-6 feet long or hexagonal. Sturdy enough to lean on and with ample room for props. (Round or longer tables make crossings and transitions more cumbersome.) Set table on a 30-degree angle, with USR corner pointing to the apex of the V.

- One chair (DSR) and a stool or second chair mirroring the footprint of the table.

- Another chair is tucked flush under the table on the US side facing audience, preset with lab coat. Dr. Wing's glasses are in easy reach in front of the chair.

- USL, a flip chart on an easel with the paper-side facing US (to not draw light bounce or draw focus). A marker and a brand-free plastic bag with snacks on the floor next to the easel. Note: if the table is big enough to allow for the easel to sit on the table without overcrowding the other props, the tripod legs can be short; otherwise, legs are telescoped out so that the easel can be placed compactly up against the SL side of table when needed. When the chart is brought in for use, it needs to be in view of most or all of the audience.

- USR corner of table: Stan's letters (except first one) separated by monologue and prefolded for easy access and management. Mitch's opened and ready snack food (a protein bar or bag of easy-chew gummies or something easy to swallow) and a bottle of water, preferably sports cap/no-spill top.

- DSL on table: Virg's ball cap and basketball.

- USL corner of table: Michael's cell phone. Note: if easel is being put on the table for monologue #7 and not on the floor, keep DSL corner clear of loose props.

- Flip chart pre-set: Leave the top sheet or two blank. Next page holds the list of Mitch's options: *Mitch talk to John. Beat up John. Talk to Jana's friends, fam, etc. Call hot line. Rescue Jana.* Write large enough to be read by the audience and with room to write in *"Talk To Jana"* at the bottom. Next page may need to be blank if the paper is see-through, but following page holds the T-chart: two columns with headers, the left labeled *STAYS*, the right labeled *LEAVES*. The left column list includes: *Loss of friends. Loss of intimacy. Could lose job/have schoolwork be affected. Could get hurt.* The right column is blank.

(Actor enters from house or from back stage as STAN THE MAN. May integrate name of community/school in a fun but quick welcome – high energy! This is his stage, and his show. He treats audience as his studio audience and as if they are recording live. Choose when to speak to camera and when to connect with audience. STAN wears sunglasses at most times.)[1]

1. STAN THE MAN

YO! Hello! Stan the Man is here to steer you clear!

[Inserts improv, sample: I say hey there, McGuffin College! Can I get a hey? I said can I get a hey! All right – there's a pulse, we're going live...!][2]

Stan The Man, here to steer you clear, to answer your questions and provide you with suggestions! You gotta little love-ly? You gettin' cudd-ly? You feeling stud-ly?

---

1 The energy at the top of the show needs to be big, explosive, attention grabbing. Stan has a big presence, easy and at home in front of a crowd. The actor needs to win over the audience with charm, speed, and confidence, especially as most teenagers are fairly sure this play is going to be didactic and boring. Any improv at the top needs to only be a few seconds, at the risk of starting on a weak footing. Think late-night-show monologues; he enjoys performing, he is confident but not a jerk. The tone of Stan's responses are as if to a younger brother who just needs a little guidance: teasing but not shaming, believing that if these letter writers just had a little more information about power, control, relationships, bullying, etc., they would do the right thing.
2 Inspired by hip-hop and spoken word, the rhythm and rhymes, internal as well as external, allow for speed, counterpoints in pauses, and line/word emphasis – all very useful in Stan's storytelling. Bring the audience along with you. It's important that the presentation of this character resonate with the actor, regardless of race or ethnicity. Historically, the Caucasian actors have struggled with how to do this role without appropriating black, urban culture, and they have found success when they trusted the musicality of the lines instead of trying to be something they are not.

You come to me, my advice is free. Stan the Man tells you straight up, no set up. Let's see what's in the mail today.

(Pulls a folded letter from pocket and reads.)

Dear Stan The Man, I've got a new girlfriend—(To center rear of house, to "camera.") Hey, congratulations!

(Spots the problem.)

Oh… complications!

(Reads.)

She's wanting to "wait" and I'm wondering how long it'll take? Signed, Andy Ticipation.

(Puts letter away. To Andy, through the camera.)

That's a dandy situation, Mr. Andy "Ticipation" and I got a good vibration you're gonna get real good at waiting, so savor the flavor of anticipating! Players, pay attention and learn something from this small demonstration for Andy Ticipation: Word 'no':

(Spin or a physical shift and pose to indicate each girl is different for each version of "no.")[3]

"No, I am not ready."

"No, 'cause you ain't prepared."

or,—Andy, son, the truth might hurt—

"No, not if you were the last man on earth."

---

[3] Definitely to get a laugh, but actually be funny by *being* each of those girls and not relying on campy, mocking, diminishing, or sexist humor of man-playing-woman. The more true the funnier it will be.

Ha! That's right! In each of these scenarios she's saying it in stereo with one common denominator, so slow down your carburetor: She said no.

Now that's the time a' day, and I got lots more to say, now we've got the a-b-c's and 1-2-3's outta the way.

Send me a letter, and we'll see if we can make it all better. Stan the Man, here to steer you clear.

> *(From C or DSR of table, puts sunglasses and letter USL corner of table. Picks up basketball[4] and puts on ball cap.[5])*

2. VIRGIN LARRY[6]

I tell ya', the way people talk about sex all the time, you'd think half the world was gettin' it daily. In the movies, it's like they kiss, and baddah-boom, you know, the next instant, they're doin' it. Come on — it's not like you can pick up a basketball and then be in the NBA.[7]

---

4   Every actor has the temptation to bounce this thing. Be aware of how it will sound on that particular floor and in that room. Don't let it obscure your lines and keep control (and if it does get away from you, find a way to use that flub to your advantage). The ball is an extension of Virg, and it will be useful later when he is trying to avoid eye contact with the audience.
5   Take time to establish a new physical center for each character: shift posture, set your jaw — which helps with vocal differentiation between characters — before turning around. Allow a beat before starting lines. Later on in the piece the transitions can be swifter, but let the audience keep up with you. Hook the audience by letting Virg see the audience seeing him, and then let him turn on the charm.
6   The name is word play on the "Virgin Mary."
7   Because that would be ridiculous. Virg likes to crack jokes, and flash his winning smile.

Now me, I was a late bloomer. I got the nickname "the Virgin Larry."[8] "Virg" for short. Yeah, pretty funny, day in and day out, *Hey, Virg – too bad you can't score in bed like you score on the court!* And if gay-dar radar's turned on you, well buckle up, buddy, 'cause it's gonna be a bumpy ride. *Hey Virg, if I ever hear you're shooting for the other team...*[9] I got the first chick into bed that I could. It went well. No. Actually, uh, actually things were a little...premature. Hey, I mean that in several ways. They call that irony. Pretty funny... You think it's been easy having the nickname the Virgin Larry?[10]

(Returns hat and ball on DR corner of table. Picks up snack, shifting body into MITCH.)

3. MITCHELL[11]

Why do some people think staying in a lousy relationship is better than being in no relationship? Why does someone who is supposed to love and care about someone else reg-

---

8 Ironic badge of honor, like calling a big guy Tiny. He has likely used this as a sympathy card with girls.
9 Differentiate the voice of these lines—he's doing an imitation of what is said to him by other guys, who are likely in a group setting where bullies like to mock people. He finds the insinuation childish but doesn't challenge the homophobic banter.
10 Virg has multiple levels here. He goes for the laugh, for the self-deprecating humor: if you laugh at yourself first, the sting is taken out of others making fun of you. And besides, at this point in his BBall career, he's one of the team, accepted and safe.
11 Mitch is every-guy's guy. Maybe not super popular, but not unpopular. Non-threatening, comfortable in his own skin, and not needing to be the center of attention. Always hungry. As with all of the monologues, especially the first time the character is introduced, the actor needs to raise the stakes—why now, what's really behind this moment and need for the character to be heard and understood by whomever it is they are talking to? Mitch tends to get a little high energy, but then has some self-awareness about it.

ularly and publicly treat them like crap? Why are relationships so complicated?

(Sees the audience seeing him getting all wound up.)

Why am I ranting? Okay. Here's the situation.

(Pulls center stool or chair DSC and sits to explain.)[12]

Eight or ten of us are hanging out. Jana and John are there. I'm probably more friends with Jana than John, but ever since they started seeing each other, John acts like Jana's his property. Anyway. She's hardly said two words this whole time, and then she offered an opinion about something. Well. John jumped all over her. Calling her all kinds of names. The nicest thing he said was, *You're an idiot; you don't know nothing. Why you wearing those jeans – they make you look fat.*[13] Whoa. What is this, grade school? He's way out of line. I'm looking around, seeing if anybody else is gonna say something here. Jana looked like she wanted to die. I had to say something. *Jana, don't put up with his lip.*[14] Well John starts jumping all over me.

(Gets up, as JOHN, addressing MITCH in front of him.)

Hey, Mr. Mitchell, what you think you're doing, hitting on my woman right in front of my face?

---

12 What he recounts has been eating at his conscience.
13 Italics signal he is speaking or recounting these lines in conversation with/as someone else, not as Mitchell. Use a different voice for John as a tough guy, but don't make John seem to be a buffoon.
14 Whenever a character is speaking directly to someone who is not visible to the audience, place the addressee for the audience and speak to that character directly as if the body was there. Don't place them off stage in the wings. Mitch's character has a lot of physical and vocal work to do to clarify when he is speaking to someone else (usually it's Jana), to the audience/his confidant, or to himself.

(MITCH isn't scared but he isn't stupid. To John.)

No, man. I just don't think you need to treat your girlfriend like that. Couple others joined in, saying he was crazy, paranoid. He took that well. Wound up storming off, dragging Jana with him, but after laying down offers to rearrange my face. Whatever. Part of me keeps saying, "Not your problem, Mitch. Mind. Your. Own. Business." But if I just stand there and pretend nothing's wrong I'm agreeing with John.

(He's at the end of his story and his snack.)

I'm going to need more of this. You want anything from the store?[15]

(Turns USC and leaves snack on the table.[16] Cross behind table DSL, picking up phone on way. Starts to dial, chickens out.)

4. MICHAEL

Do you realize that everything considered "feminine," "unmanly," that's everything it takes to be a good father? Father. Jana's called me dada, daddy, dad, then, when her mother and I divorced, Michael. I used to say that when

---

15 Actors have usually thrown in an ad lib here directly addressing an audience member—asking something like, "Power bar? Okay." This is another hook into the audience and it will pay off later.
16 Assigning specific types of entrances or crossings and even general areas on the stage for each character helps not only the actor to make the physical transition and to develop body memory of what character is next, it greatly aids the audience in recognizing the character the next time they come around, even before a word is said. This can also be accomplished with a physical sign in—a lift of the belt, a scratch on the head, or some other tick that has been found as useful for the characterization. It was always fun and magical to watch an actor quickly shift his core and morph.

Jana got to be the dating age I'd…I'd…well, she wouldn't be dating. Well. Now I'm lucky if I even get to meet any of her friends. There's a very independent young woman who lives at the other end of this phone.

(Dial and wait for the call to be picked up.)

Jana, hi, it's Michael. Uh, how are you?[17]

(Jana does not give him much time or slack.)

Good! Good! …well, no, it's just, uh, I just haven't seen much of you lately – you seem to spend most of your free time with John…[18] *Uh, I know, he's your boyfriend…Uh… How are things going with him?*

(To audience)

Oh no, my little girl isn't old enough to have sex yet, maybe when she's thirty, thirty-five —

(To Jana)

Why?

(To audience)

Why?

(To Jana)

Becaaaauusssse, because I wanted to know if – if you two – wanted to go to – to the zoo – or to get some ice cream – sometime.

---

17 In this short phone call Michael is aware of so many things: he's been afraid to call, he's desperate to call, it's been too long, he's behaving badly, she is grown up, he could lose her.
18 He can't help himself, and he tries not to sound too wounded or petulant.

(To audience)

Did I really just say that?

(Pivot and reverse entrance, replacing the phone on USL corner of table and putting on WING's glasses and lab coat as starting next monologue. Continue the cross as an arc behind the table to DSC. He addresses the audience as his class.)

5. DR. WING[19]

Okay, class: have you any questions before tomorrow's exam?

(As if an individual in the audience has asked this question.)

Ah, no, Tony, I don't really like the nickname "Dr. Wing-ding." Simply "Dr. Wing" will be fine, thank you! Are there questions about the exam…? No? All right then, except for Jana. *(To her)* — I need to talk to you about your paper — class is dismissed a little early today. Thank you all. Study hard. Ah, Jana, have a seat[20] and let me find your paper[21]…

---

19 Most actors have made Wing a little geeky, which isn't to say weak. Wing is very comfortable as a man whose best muscle is his brain, and he enjoys his persona as a professor: it takes a special kind of energy to be a successful teacher, and to be respected enough to be teased by his students, and confident enough to enjoy it and dish it back. He is earnest, which is part of his charm. For adults — parents, co-workers, bosses, people who work with youth — Wing demonstrates a safe intervention.
20 Making the cross back to the table, find the right moment to move or indicate the center chair or stool for Jana to sit. As Wing is going to be talking to the air, it helps the audience to place where she is.
21 A deliberately casual public statement. If John sees that everyone is out of class and he does not see Jana, Wing has established a plausible reason and witnesses. Wing has thought this conversation like a scientist, with great care and contingency plans. Wing recognized that John considers a change in schedule an offense for which Jana can be punished.

(Behind his chair, he rifles through things on his desk.)

No, no, we ended early today, so we should have a few minutes before your boyfriend, who drops you off and picks you up after class each and every day, gets here.[22]

(WING steps flat across SR to his classroom "door" that the students have just filed out, USR to off-stage. He looks both ways down the hall before the mimed action of closing the door.) [23]

Please, Jana, sit down for just a moment.

(Indicates the center chair or stool and "hands" Jana her paper.)[24]

Ah, I didn't really want to talk about your paper. Well, yes, in a manner of speaking, something's wrong[25]…this is awkward. While my job is to teach science, the curriculum and my syllabus aren't more important than the Homo sapiens exchanging carbon dioxide for oxygen in front of me…

(Weak. He's as uncomfortable as she is. Crosses to his desk, staying DS)

---

22 An observation; not snarky or judgmental, but the point won't be lost on the audience.
23 Consider that when Wing closes the door, some people will have alarm and worry that he is going to be creepy or inappropriate, and this is not who Wing is.
24 As Jana is invisible to the audience, help the audience be aware of where her body is, establish her height, and look at eye-level when looking at her directly. Too low and it looks like you're staring at her chest. Keeping the plane of Wing's chin high helps, as does handing Jana her (invisible) paper. While she needs to be established, keep the audience focus on Wing by limiting and choosing with care when to look at Jana. Make those moments brief because on a technical level, an audience looking at the actor looking at nothing doesn't work; and, on an interpersonal level, staring at Jana is threatening.
25 Sits down somewhere in here. Important to pointedly first shift the chair a little away from Jana—don't crowd her space—and face front. Note that the established door to offstage is now behind him, USR. No manspreading!

Jana, I can't ignore my students when... well... Do you remember two classes ago you were a few minutes late finishing up a lab—oh no, don't apologize. However, I observed that your boyfriend John was very unhappy with having to wait for you and then—no—no, Jana, no, that was not your fault. You did not make him get upset. John chose to get upset. This was not a question of you being at fault, this was a case of—of...[26] I saw John grab you by the elbow, here, and twist. The words he used as he removed you from this classroom were not kind. Please, last class I noticed you had bruises—no, no, you're right—

> *(Jana is frightened and is ready to bolt. Having anticipated this, crosses to the door.)*[27]

I'm sure you don't want to talk to your lab professor about your personal life. That's precisely why I had waited until today to approach you.[28] Do you know the student bulletin board by the elevators? There's a poster for a local agency. It has a phone number on the bottom. Or, in the front of any phone book, or these days on-line, you can find several hotlines numbers.

I'm worried about you, Jana, and—

---

26 Beat shifts. He is honest and concerned, but matter-of-fact, not judgemental.
27 Find the right spot to cross back to the door without getting too close to Jana or threateningly blocking her access to the door—the tension is that she does want to leave and he's not done with what he needs to say.
28 Find a spot in here to sit down next to Jana again. Face front with his back to the door. Regarding what he's saying: he obviously made sure this poster was there. The first version of the play had him hand her a note (which was as invisible as her paper) but we realized that if John had entered and caught this action, or found the phone number on her, it could be dangerous for Jana.

> *(Quick double-take over right shoulder as John has burst in. WING stays calm and welcoming to John, whose hostility is inferred.)*

Ah! Hello, John! You're right on time to pick up Jana![29] — Come in, come in — no — this isn't a private conversation — Jana will be right with you.[30] So, as I was saying, you may have to adjust your paper's formatting, but I suggest you submit it for the department scholarship — and I really think you've explained the moral complexity of stem cell research with great clarity. You can speak to the department chair for more information.

> *("Remembering" that he is busy, WING acknowledges them both[31] and crosses to behind his desk chair.)*

Now, if you two will excuse me, I need to prepare for my next class. I hope you both have a pleasant day.[32]

> *(Leaves lab coat on the chair and glasses on the table. Picks up STAN's sunglasses and next letters, lands DSC.)*

6. STAN THE MAN[33]

We're back with a stack. It's time to find what's on your mind!

---

29 Coming off as snarky could put John on alert and risk putting Jana in danger of physical harm.
30 When he turns his attention to Jana, and turns his back on John, he can casually but firmly signal to Jana with his normalcy that she needn't panic.
31 Give these invisible people extra wide berth when crossing to the table.
32 He watches them go out before he drops his cover of calm. He is worried.
33 Stan brings welcome levity to follow the seriousness of Wing's encounter. Take transition time to to address the camera and the studio audience. This section gets more serious as the letters get more serious.

(Reads.)

Dear Stan The Man, if I buy a girl dinner, I wanna go home a winner. Any advice?

(To studio camera.)

Listen up; I'm not saying it twice. Mr. Un-Happy Meal, here's how I feel: dinner's a date not a deal. It's not too late! Just get real.

(Reads next letter.[34])

Stan the Man, I could use some help around this place, when you gonna call your poor old neglected mothe –

(Catching on and appreciating that he's been punked, at work, on TV, by his mother and the crew.)

Look, Ma, I'm busy – who let this through? I'll call you this weekend, Moms, I promise. Next letter!

(Reads.)

Dear Stan the Man, a friend of mine is in a violent relationship. He's afraid to get help, and he's afraid to leave…how do you help a friend who is gay and not out, get out of danger?

Heterosexual, bisexual, transgender, gay, lesbian, questioning – it's a situation wanting liberation, adjusting. Safety first. Get him through the worst one step at a time. My advice, call the local hotline. He needs a personalized plan, not just Stan the Man. Follow up, all right?[35]

---

34 Manage these props so they don't distract the audience.
35 The response to this letter is not a canned answer, he had to work for it. It is not a blow-off. He acknowledges the seriousness of this situation, and importantly, his own limitations. There *is* a time to involve police or authorities.

(Reads.)

Stan the Man – I thought it was true love forever, but we broke up, and I'm being tagged in some embarrassing photos online – and people have written some ugly things. And still worse, my ex's friends are making it personal, trolling all my social media.

Today swipe right—yeah that's all right; now this beau, this photo—yeah, that's fine but tomorrow maybe you gotta redefine the line, 'cause someone dropped into psycho on a dime. How can a smile so sweet, flip the switch, be the creep you can't delete? Virtual reality, virtually impossible to undo, like a tattoo you wish you could re-do, maybe even take back the I-love-you. The world-wide-web is not private your-space—it's a public chase. Catch yourself a bully, get a stalker's disrespect… it's technology feeding ugly pathology, electronic punches with no apology. Hey, I'm sorry. Remove the tags, maybe take down your site. Re-think how you your document your night. Threats and defamation? Take it to the station.[36]

> *(Crosses up center, returns sunglasses and letters. A beat, then dash USR for flipchart, marker, and bag with snacks. Flip chart either is on the table or tight against the DSL corner of the table.)*

7. MITCHELL

Okay. Welcome to the think tank! I've got protein bars here for those who think it'll help.

---

36 The increasing seriousness of the letters may lead to a heaviness—that can be countered by Stan's recognition that he's doing the work that needs to be done.

> [Insert improv[37] : (Sample) Sorry, they were out of Mountain Dew. And that rots your stomach lining you know.]
>
> (Steps DS, away from table.)

Now. A friend of mine, Jana, is in an abusive and increasingly dangerous relationship.

> (Focus snaps, as if in response to a comment from an audience member.)

What? You think I'm over-reacting? Well, last night at a party John put his fist through a wall, about an inch to the right of Jana's head. *(A beat.)* It's time for me to do something. So! What are my options? This is what I've got so far.

> (Steps to easel, flips top pages to reveal list.)[38]

Mitch talk to John. Uh, no, as he's not open to friendly constructive criticism, and definitely not from me. *Beat up John.* Sure. *(An implied bad idea.)* I don't want to risk making him even madder, and put Jana in even more danger.

Talk to Jana's friends etc.[39] Get this—I talked to one of Jana's friends who thought she'd convinced her to break up with John. Well. The next day, you know what happened. Jana

---

37 Relate it to the improv at the end of his first monologue.
38 Adjust the chart to make sure most of audience can see it. Can step down and away from chart as he thinks through the options, returning focus to the chart for each new idea. It sounds obvious, but make clear choices on when to read off the page and when to address audience, and don't block the list with your body. If sight lines are bad, just alternate where you stand so the chart isn't blocked the whole time.
39 This item could include family and roommate or teammate or sorority sisters, if there is something that would resonate for that audience.

went right back to him. That makes it kinda hard to be friends after that, you know.

Call hotline. But "hotline" makes it sound like life and death.

> (*Uncomfortable truth.*)

Rescue Jana. Yeah. Chivalry. I'll just get a white horse, ride on in, and? Then what? She may not want to be rescued, and John's not gonna just sit back and let that happen. She wanted to leave a *party* and he punched a hole in the wall. What's he going to do when she wants to leave *him*?

> (*A more uncomfortable truth.*)

So what are my options?

> (*Returns to the list, weighs choices. Works his way up the list from the bottom to cross off* Rescue, Beat up, *and* Talk to John. *Circles or checks good options.*)

No. No. No. Okay, yeah, I can check in with other people, see what they know... Okay, I'll call that number. Or! Better yet! I'll make Jana call, and maybe they can... Listen to me. I'm just someone else trying to push Jana around. I don't even know what she wants to do.

> (*Truth dawns.*)

RIGHT!

> (*Rushes back to add to the chart.*)

Talk... to... Jana.[40]

---

40 This pleases Mitch, and how nice that his posse of friends — the audience — could help him work through a next course of action!

(Leaves marker on table.[41] *From CS, full back to audience for transition, with Officer Friendly physical sign-in — a hitch of the belt, scratch of head? — and crosses behind the SR chair, wide circle DSR.)*

8. OFFICER FRIENDLY[42]

Did you know that approximately 73%[43] of all rape is committed by friends, family members, and acquaintances?[44] Apparently, it's not that masked stranger in a dark alley that a woman, man, or child has to fear as much as they have to fear the smiling faces around them. That's a conversation stopper all right. My name is Officer Friendly. And yes, that would be my real name.[45]

---

41 If you are following this blocking, you will see arcs, 8s and circles. If you can have Mitch finish so it is easy to step back to the center sweet spot, it will allow room for a full transformation to Officer Friendly. While some of the earlier transitions may be getting shorter, this is the first time we meet Friendly. Taking time to find his center, his walk, and establishing this cross behind the two chairs/stool as his signature entrance is helpful.

42 This character has evolved over time, and new lines in upcoming monologues have helped to make him less flat and stereotypical. Similar to Wing, he has a room full of people in front of him that he has to convince that they want to hear what he has to say. Though he carries himself as someone who has had training in protecting and serving, making him too barky, too military, or even too clowny (condescending!) can be self-sabotage. Over-aggressive portrayal could spark resistance from an audience, whether because they are feeling defensive or afraid or because this talk about violence and abuse is a little too close to what is going on at home or with their friends. Similar to how Stan approaches his audience, Friendly knows that treating this audience with respect, with the belief they are that "mass in the middle" who are not perpetrators, that they are people who want to do the right thing,. Own the DSR/C front of the stage, with a few steps to the left or right, avoiding pacing. Your chin and eyeballs can help hold your audience. Consider that he would never give his back to the audience while speaking to them — that is too vulnerable a position.

43 Check for most current stat.

44 Each of these questions is a hook to engage with your scene partner/audience.

45 His attitude and sense of irony here can take tension or resistance down a notch.

Now, in every audience there's always someone who has a story. The same story. Every audience. *Excuse me, sir, but I know a guy whose life was ruined when he was falsely accused of rape by a woman wanting to get revenge.* To which I reply that there's no statistical difference between falsely reported rape and falsely reported crime in general. True fact. More often, rape goes unreported. Also true.

Now, why would a rape go unreported?[46] Good question. Remember, I told you about that 73%? Friends, family members, dating partners? As for those who believe the victim must have "asked for it," no. No one is ever asking to be raped, and blaming the victim isn't a helpful strategy. As for falsely claiming rape to get revenge, weeeellll, actually, there're more expedient ways of seeking revenge—

    (Almost an aside; catching himself.)

—which I decline to go into, in the interest of promoting non-violence.[47]

    (He's ended CS. Turns around to get cap and ball, pivot as VIRG.)

---

46 This line as if someone in the audience just asked, but don't pause to pretend it happened in real time.

47 Levity. Give the man a break—this is a thankless job!

9. VIRGIN LARRY[48]

Fall sports at this school include sex and drugs and alcohol and seein' how many firsties you can score before the playoffs. So far the season's had a good start. The Virgin Larry's become remarkably smooth! I set up the approach, dodge the defense, anticipate the side escape, and three points, touchdown, homerun, score! Don't look at me that way, cause that's how you tell the story if anybody wants to know. And they always do.[49]

A buddy of mine, probably my best friend, Tom, Tom the Terminator he's called. Unstoppable on the court. Team captain. One time he got in some trouble—this girl was saying he raped her. I asked him, I said Tom, tell me straight. Hey, if he said he didn't do it, then I believe he didn't do it. He's my man.[50] That girl was sorry she ever brought it up.[51]

Well, a few days ago Tom was saying that he's got a "home video" for the team to see after practice. A little way into watching it, it's clear the girl—the girl, she don't have any idea she's on candid camera, much less that she's gonna be on display for the entire basketball team's play-by-play

---

48 The audience could use a little levity at this point. Take a moment to be Virg, to charm them, to be the lighthearted, fun guy he is when he isn't trying to fit in. The lighter he can be at the top of this monologue, the more you can open the hearts of the audience and increase the intensity of this devastating story of witnessing a video-taped rape. Consider what Virg is *not* saying throughout this monologue. His habits and fidgeting with the ball and his cap can help tell the story.
49 Perhaps not aware of the double standard, but he is painfully aware of social pressure and locker room talk.
50 The code of loyalty.
51 He has not yet clocked that he was complicit and a culpable participant in the backlash against this girl.

review. She also, well, she also said stop or wanted him to stop, a few times, but Tom, unstoppable Tom the Terminator had selective hearing that night. Oh boy. *Go, go go, Tom, go, you the man, Tom you the man you-the-man, you-the-man...*[52] Yeah, Tom. You the man.

Anyway. Within a few days that girl figured out she missed the private screening. I—I had forgotten about that other girl, from before. I'm wondering if maybe back then I was just believing who I wanted to believe, you know?

> *(Replaces hat and ball on table, exchanging for snack. Repeats the first entrance as MITCH, crossing USR behind the chairs. Rounding the corner, he sees the audience observing him and his snack.)*

10. MITCHELL[53]

Now I'm just eating because I'm nervous.

> *(Rids the snack at the table, and gets a sip of water if needed, then steps DSC.)*

Jana does her studying at the library while John's at work. I decide to talk to her there. When John won't be around.[54]

> *(Place Jana DSL as if seated.)*

---

52 Transition this beat to re-enact the mob mentality of the guys watching the rape unfold. Virg's cracks—his attempt to keep it together—are palpable in his breath, speech pattern, and eye contact (or lack of) which carry him through this monologue. This is difficult for Virg to say and it is difficult for the audience to hear.

53 The humor of this monologue helps undercut how scary it is to approach someone with your concerns about their safety or well-being. Fast-paced and very physical, Mitch flips from talking to Jana, to talking to the audience, to conveying what Jana says to Mitch. We should always know which.

54 Smart idea. This will not burden her, raise flags, or alter her schedule.

Jana's at a study table.

> *(Gathers courage for the approach, and leans to talk to Jana.)*

Jana. Hi. Howerya doing? Hey, I'm glad I found you… I, uh— *(To audience)* I don't know what I'm doing—I just jump in. *(To Jana)* I'd like to talk with you for a minute because, uh… see, I'm worried about — *(To audience)* She cuts me off. "Sorry but I'm studying here. That table is free."[55] Okay…

> *(Confused but she's given him no invitation or option, MITCH crosses to sit on SR chair or the stool.)*

A minute or so goes by and she walks to the water fountain and drops a note next to me.

> *(Picks it up and reads.)*

Meet me in the 700 stacks in three minutes, but don't leave when I do and go a different way. What's this, a James Bond movie?

> *(Action of checking his watch for appointed time. Cross DSL — Jana's study table area is now the book stacks — and the action of finding the right number and aisle, looking upstage, down stage, upstage, whispering for Jana. Flat cross DS from R to L serves to place MITCH essentially back in front of the chair he had been sitting in. Looking upstage, she startles him from behind. He jumps and places Jana just to his left.)*

Jana, hey, what's with this spy-meets-spy stuff? She says John's friends report to him who she talks to, "because he's jealous of other guys. He's protective that way." *This is abusive.* She says, "John's not abusive. He loves me. He'd

---
[55] As with Stan's use of the female voices in the opening monologue, Mitch is story-telling here, so the voice should not mock or be distracting.

never hit me." This kind of behavior is abusive. Having friends track who you talk to is abusive. Not being able to talk to who you want to... *Jana, even if he hasn't hit you, this controlling crap, putting you down in front of people, it's like he is hitting you but no one can see those marks. And hey, what about the hole in the wall, the one he punched next to your head?* She looked startled, but she defended him. She says I don't know him like she does, that I don't understand what he's been through, that I "don't see how tender, loving, and generous he can be." *I'm sure he's got his good points, Jana, I mean you wouldn't go out with a guy who – ah, it's just –* She says she has to go now.[56] *Jana, I want you to know that I'm here if you ever need someone to listen.* She said, "If you're that concerned for me, you won't make it worse." And she left. Great. So she knows it can get worse. Great.

> (Circles behind chair from DSR to UC to retrieve sunglasses and last letter from the table. He encourages the nods of recognition as the audience realizes this is STAN. Takes the DSC sweet-spot.)

11. STAN THE MAN[57]

Dear Stan The Man, what if a guy and a girl are both drinking, and they have sex? Later she says she hadn't wanted to, but was too messed up to be able to say stop. I say that she was drinking

---

56 Jana is out of patience and Mitch is out of time. He has to get this following statement in before she takes off.
57 This monologue is dead center for the show, flanked by Virg's bomb and Dad's bomb-out with Jana. The musicality of this speech helps carry the intensity of emotion. Breath. Space. Speed. Pause to let the imagery sink in.

and shouldn't have been drunk if she didn't want to fool around, but my friend Joe says that's rape. Thanks for steering us clear.[58]

(Tucks the letter away in his pocket.)

No problem. That's why I'm here. Your man Joe knows which way the wind blows, what the rules are. The "we-were-both-drinking" thinking—that's a trap not gettin' you far: If you're drunk driving it's a matter-o-fact it's who's driving the car sits behind the bars—not your friend passed out inside you took for a ride!

(Starts to leave, but one more thought to the camera.)

It's a tragedy if you ain't capable of sympathy, don't know empathy, can't imagine bein' in someone else's skin.

(Idea has formed. Removes sunglasses and engages the audience directly for much of this, keeping them on the hook.)

It's time to step in.

Imagine this. Imagine your sister, your mother, one good friend or another.[59] Maybe you're on the telephone, maybe you're both alone…Okay, now: She says she's got something important to say, she's seeing shades of grey, she needs you to listen and not go away. You hear her fear,

---

58 This letter carries forward the arc of the letters which are becoming increasingly serious. He will need to take his time to figure out how to respond, but still keep the audience hooked.

59 This is addressing the "mass in the middle" again. Conveying this as an example of empathy is only one way to have this conversation, and it has limitations. It is not effective logic with people who have dehumanized their sister, mother, one good friend or another with abuse, violence, or objectification; for those who feel entitled to someone's body; with cultural or religious systems that privilege power over others; or, when narcissism or unchecked personality disorders override civility and consideration. That said, empathy supports a victim, and may inspire further action.

and she's got your ear. She's got a friend, charming and smart, who's been after her heart. She tells you something bad happened, she thinks, that maybe she had had a little too much to drink — or maybe she had nothing to drink — and she tells you they were getting a little friendly. Cut to where she's saying no. She pushes his hand away. He tries again anyway. She says no, number two. He tries again. Now what's he gonna do? And this time as he's crossin' the line, she stays really quiet and still and he thinks he's gotta green light to cruise down this hill. He's not slowin'. He keeps goin'. She already said no-no-no but all that's in his head is go-go-go.

Doctor's analysis, she's got paralysis, she can only watch it, she can't stop it.

This is making war, not love: I can't tell you more. G is for "green," G is for "go," but the G is silent in "that's enough." This is your sister, or your friend… and yeah I'll end.

> *(If not DSC, steps to. Sunglasses back on. "Camera" time but no need for pomp.)*

Removing illusions, avoiding confusions. Empathy, like sympathy only better. Stan the Man. Thanks for the letter.

> *(Returns glasses and letter to table. Quick cross behind table — as before — putting phone to ear as rounding corner behind table to DS.)*

12. MICHAEL

(Speaking to Jana's mother, his ex-wife.)

So Jana hasn't told you about this either? Look — I understand you're upset — believe me — I — Can we put our issues aside and focus on Jana? I'll call you as soon as I talk to her. Yes. I will. Goodbye —

(She's said something that moves him.)

…I know. Me too.

(Hangs up. He's upset and winds himself up further.)

Her mother and I hardly ever see her, so how could we know? I have to have some friend of Jana's tell me what's going on.[60] My job is to take care of her. What I don't understand is how this has happened. How did it get to this point?[61] I didn't realize. I've let her down. I didn't realize it could hurt so much. She's got to get out of this.[62]

(Composes himself, redials.)

Jana, it's Mich — it's your father. Is this a good time? We need to talk —

(Spins US[63] to leave phone on the SR chair. Sign in, repeat FRIENDLY's cross behind the chairs to deploy his question-to-the-audience strategy.)

---

60 Could this be Mitch who gave Michael heads up?
61 Michael catches himself victim-blaming.
62 This is one of the most emotionally dense passages in the script. The rapi flow of feelings — shame, guilt, anger, fear, shame — cycle through with a word or even a syllable.
63 End with a strong pose or profile, such as hand on the hip and phone to ear with elbow extended. This will give a visual cue to the next time Dad signs in.

13. OFFICER FRIENDLY

Now, if a person's been raped, they'd know it, right? Sadly, it's not so simple as it sounds. What if rape is unrecognized by the victim because of alcohol or drug use? What if they've been raped by someone they've previously been intimate with? Frankly, there's no mention in the US Constitution of the right to have sex with someone who is unwilling. Even if they are married or dating.

You know,[64] people always want to know why I do this — what fool in their right mind would stand up in front of crowds of young adults and start dishing up facts and statistics about sexual assault?

The "People-magazine-reality-TV-mentality" would need me to tell you that my sister was raped, raped and killed, and because of that, I've made it my mission to go out and spread the word. Maybe.

Or maybe there's a young transgender person who has been harassed and I'm coming to the rescue wearing a badge of tolerance and equality. Maybe.

Or it could be the department was tipped off because someone is dropping date-rape drugs at parties. Maybe.

Now any of that, or none of that, could be why I do this. But not one of us, myself included, has to wait for the excuse of something terrible happening before we act like we care.

---

64 Friendly gets real. Beat change. He speaks as a human and not as an authority figure.

(Pivot and step for VIRG's ball and cap, character transformation completed in the circle. VIRG can't find his words right away — nor can he look people in the eye the way he could before. He works his way DS.)

14. VIRGIN LARRY

Basketball. The great analogy for life. Boundaries, rules, referees.[65] I think most guys are waiting for a ref to blow the whistle on a foul, and no whistle… *(Shrugs.[66])* Except this time I wasn't even on the court and there was no whistle. Just a phone call from the athletic director. The girl in Tom's "home movie" went to the police. The school is reviewing the whole situation and possible expulsions for everyone who was there, and they might revoke all our athletic scholarships.[67] But me. Me. I did nothing — nothing! Nothing to stop it.

(Swaps ball and cap for Wing's glasses.)

---

65 This is the code. This is Virg's entire world structure. It is completely crumbling around him.
66 If you don't get caught it didn't happen, right? Sometimes actors do a controlled roll of the ball off or back stage, symbolic as well as leaving Virg without the security of his ball.
67 He's angry, he's scared, and he knows he blew it. The recogntion of potential loss of the scholarship is a watershed moment: there is now life marked as before they got caught, and life marked as after. No need to rush the end of this monologue — let the reality of being in deep trouble settle in with the audience.

15. DR. WING [68]

My first lab partner in college…mmm…chemistry at first sight.[69] It ended in heartbreak; mine. I finally discovered why she wouldn't, well, couldn't trust me. She had been abused, emotionally and then later physically, by her first dating partner. It would take her years to ever trust again. Violence is a chain reaction,[70] and what he did to her, in turn, continues to impact and hurt others. And that's why I spoke out to Jana.

> *(Swaps glasses for phone from SR chair, and assumes last pose as dad, turning his back to audience. We see that Jana has hung up on him. He takes his time with the phone, not wanting to make eye contact, but he has to. Sits. Attempts to keep it together.)*

16. MICHAEL

So. I wanted to say…

> *(Deliver to an audience member as stand-in for Jana.)*

…I am your father and I would do anything to have you be happy. I know I can't live your life for you; that you have to make your own choices. But even if you are all grown up, you're not alone. If you ever need to talk to me, I will listen. I will

---

68 At this point in the arc of the performance there is balance between surfing the energy in the room and the pacing in the play. Find where to pause to let people catch up to the story being told, where to build in emotional beats, where to accelerate, and where to compress. All of this to signal that the play is wrapping up. But don't rush it!
69 Yes. He knows this is a terrible joke. Light touch of levity helps both the actor and the audience here.
70 A scientific albeit simplistic lens: Cause-effect.

always believe you. I will always love you. I will not judge you. Let me in.

But what I said instead was—

(Resumes the position on the phone with Jana.)

—Dammit, Jana, why didn't you tell me?[71]

(Leaves phone when the beat is finished. As MITCH, gets marker from the table before addressing audience.)

17. MITCHELL

I called the local hotline. I told them my name was Horatio Sebastian Philip III.[72] They told me right away that this was an anonymous, confidential call, and I didn't need to worry. So I said I had this friend I was trying to help, and then they said, yeah, guys can be abused by their girlfriends, and I said no, I don't have a girlfriend, and then they said, well gay men also experience abusive relationships, and I said, *no*, really, this is about my friend who is a girl but not my girlfriend. Anyway, I told them the situation and they talked me through Jana's "risk analysis."

(Flips to reveal a T-Chart.)

The list of what happens if she decides to stay[73] is essentially the same list of what happens if she decides to leave.

---

71 Heads nodding in the audience for this line.
72 This passage is the last funny one, and gives the audience a chance to breathe.
73 Not so subtle reminder that it is Jana's choice. Those in an abusive relationship understand the risks better than anyone else.

(Drawing arrows from the text on the left to the empty spaces on the right of the T-chart as he reads.)

…Loss of friends. Loss of intimacy. Could lose job or have schoolwork be affected. Could get hurt. And the bad news is that the time Jana's in most physical danger is when she decides to leave.[74] If Jana calls them, they can help her set up a safety plan. A safety plan?[75] I called the hotline because I wanted to get some answers. It was good to hear I'd been doing things right, yeah, but… there's no quick fix.

(Caps marker and quick cross to exchange for sunglasses. No letter. STAN takes his DSC mark.)

18. STAN THE MAN

You're probably wondering how I got to be so smart, why I play this part, how I got this attitude. All right. I'll give you a clue.

(Glasses off.)

I watched my father beat my mother. And then he would drag her to their bedroom.[76] My mother couldn't leave him, and she couldn't press charges. The cops stopped coming.[77]

(Glasses back on – he's the performer again.)

My father is yelling,

---

74 Let the horrible possibility sink in, drop the focus on the chart, and return to face audience.
75 Mitch has mixed emotions from this information, but don't undercut the importance of a safety plan.
76 Let audience find the subtext of him being a child of rape.
77 He is not playing for sympathy. He has told us why he does what he does.

my mother is screaming,
then silence,
I'm relieved.
But there's no telling
if my ma was crying
that time I was conceived.

>(Glasses on the stool or table, signs in as FRIENDLY.)

19. OFFICER FRIENDLY

If it were your mother or your daughter, your sister or your brother or your friend, you would want justice to the fullest extent of the law.

And if it's ever you, get yourself the help you need. Do it for yourself. Do it so there's not a next victim.

>(Pivot to table for hat and ball.)

20. VIRGIN LARRY

I did nothin' to stop it, and I didn't think about leaving, and that means I'm not an innocent bystander. It doesn't seem fair. But, I gotta ask, how fair is it to be raped? If maybe I had stood up and left, then maybe others would've too, and then, then just Tom would be the one wondering what he should have done differently.

>(Pivot to trade for WING glasses.)

21. DR. WING

I could turn away and just teach my class. But I can't. What if next time John does more than bruise Jana?

> *(Leaves glasses, trade for cell phone. Allow enough time with phone to establish this is MICHAEL, and step DSC. A full beat before addressing audience.)*

22. MICHAEL

I need help keeping my daughter safe. Who will help me? Please.

> *(After the beat, a quick turn and shift to MITCH. Grabs the marker and rips the T-Chart off the pad and shoves it out of the way. Writes large on the blank page: LISTEN. Recapping the marker, steps DS to face audience.)*

23. MITCHELL

All I can do is speak up when something isn't right. And I can *listen* to Jana, give support, not judge. Give her time.

> *(Leaves marker, pivot to get sunglasses.)*

24. STAN THE MAN

In this time, in my words and my rhyme, I've shed some light on what's wrong and what's right. It's time for the violence to end, and it starts with you and your friends. But Stan the Man can't hold your hand. You the man—and yeah, Ladies, too… Now. What you gonna do? *(Exits.)*[78]

---

[78] Let the question hang. Depending on the venue, sometimes this exit is a full walk off stage; however, in some venues it's practical to simply step upstage, take a beat to drop the character, and return DS for a bow, having removed the sunglasses. If exiting the stage, return quickly for a bow—don't make them wait. The bow is a necessary signal that the performance portion of the program is done.

CHARACTER SEQUENCE FIRST/LAST LINE

This list is a convenient tool for actors in memorizing the script. As a means of building muscle memory, include the use of props and transition lines preceding and following each monologue. This will inform the overall rhythm of the play. Actors generally have used this practice as a warm up and way to test their blocking for each new venue.

1. STAN: Stan the Man... / Send me a letter...

2. VIRGIN LARRY: I tell ya, the way people talk... / Having the nickname the Virgin Larry?

3. MITCHELL: Why do some people... / You want anything from the store?

4. MICHAEL: Do you realize... / Did I really say that?

5. DR. WING: Okay class, any questions... / ...I hope you both have a pleasant day.

6. STAN: We're back with a stack... / Threats and defamation? Take it to the station.

7. MITCHELL: Welcome to the think tank... / Right! Talk. To. Jana.

8. OFFICER FRIENDLY: Did you know... / ...which I decline to go into in the interest of promoting nonviolence.

9. VIRGIN LARRY: Fall sports... / I'm wondering if back then I was just believing who I wanted to believe, you know?

10. MITCH: Now I'm just eating because I'm nervous… / She knows it can get worse. Great.

11. STAN: Dear Stan the Man: What if a guy… / Empathy like sympathy, only better. Stan the Man. Thanks for the letter.

12. MICHAEL: Jana hasn't told you about this either? / It's your father. Is this a good time? We need to talk.

13. OFFICER FRIENDLY: Now, if a person's been raped… / But not one of us, myself included, need to wait for something bad to happen before we act like we care.

14. VIRGIN LARRY: Basketball. The great analogy for life… / But me, I did nothing. Nothing. I did nothing to stop it.

15. DR WING: My fist lab partner in college… / That's why I spoke out to Jana.

16. MICHAEL: So I wanted to say… / Dammit, Jana! Why didn't you tell me?

17. MITCH: I called the local hotline… / It's good to hear I've been doing things right, yeah, but… there's no quick fix.

18. STAN: You probably wondering… / …if my ma was crying that time I was conceived.

19. OFFICER FRIENDLY: If it were your… / …do it so there's not a next victim

20. VIRGIN LARRY: I did nothing to stop it… / …and just Tom would be the one wondering what he should've done differently.

21. DR WING: I could turn away… / What if the next time, John does more than bruise Jana?

22. MICHAEL: I need help…

23. MITCH: All I can do…

24. STAN: In this time…

ACTOR PROP & TRAVEL CHECKLIST

You will find a routine if you tour the show with any frequency but keep a checklist, especially if you are your own stage manager.

PACK TO TRAVEL

- ___ Shirt, pants, belt, shoes
- ___ Stan sunglasses & letters
- ___ Mitch water, snacks, shopping bag, flip chart w/stand and clips, marker (wide, black or blue)
- ___ Virg basketball & ball cap
- ___ Michael phone
- ___ Wing glasses & lab coat
- ___ Regular and emergency contact information for site coordinator
- ___ All travel documents (ID, directions, confirmation numbers, etc.)
- ___ Copies of moderator and panel materials (often needed!)

ON-SITE

Arrive as arranged and at least one hour in advance; call ahead to reassure coordinator if there are any changes or problems.

- ___ Sound and light check
- ___ Green room
- ___ Moderator and panel check-in
- ___ Re-set props after run-through or warm-up

PRE-SET

On person:

___ Letter #1, sunglasses, hands-free microphone

On table:

___ Snack, water bottle
___ Basketball/cap
___ Remaining prepped letters, folded, separated, stacked
___ Lab coat (on chair) and glasses
___ Cell phone

On floor, USL:

___ Bag with snacks, marker. Easel with flip chart & two pre-written pages. (Leave one or two blank sheets on top and in between if paper is see-thru.)

First sheet, list:

- Mitch talk to John
- Beat up John
- Talk to Jana's friends, etc
- Call hotline
- Rescue Jana

(*Space at bottom to write in* Talk To Jana)

Second sheet, draw a T-Chart labeled with **Stays** *(left) column and* **Leaves** *(right) column. Write in this list under the* **Stays** *column:*

- Isolation
- He won't change
- Loss of friends, job
- Unsafe
- Loss of intimacy
- Could get hurt

SITE COORDINATOR CHECKLIST

___ Coordinate with local domestic violence and sexual assualt agencies to confirm date.

___ Double check performance and scheduling conflicts: bells, intercoms, sporting events, school events.

___ Provide actor with travel arrangements (as applicable):
   1. Flight reservations
   2. Airport pickup/return
   3. Lodging arrangements
   4. Directions to performance site
   5. Parking information

___ Provide actor with your preferred as well as emergency contact information (this is important!).

___ Provide actor with information about the venue, size of audience, panel, and other relevant arrangements.

___ Secure a moderator, panel members, and DV/SA professionals for post-show debriefing.

___ Plan logistics for post-show talkback, e.g., arrange for and prepare facilitators for small group discussions, assign adults to be in "trouble zones" during performance.

___ Supply moderator panel members facilitators with **The Role of the Moderator, Moderator Script, Tips for the Moderator and Panelists,** and *You the Man* **Plot Summary,** plus directions, parking info, etc., in advance of the performance day.

___ Secure safe room and resources to be available for crisis intervention (not always used, but important).

___ Get an audience! Coordinate with groups, community leaders, agencies, e.g., sororities and athletics, programs with psycholgy and health professions.

___ Prepare a playbill (printed program) to include information about the play and your local panelists, helplines, resources, and thanks to any sponsors.
   1. Title: You the Man by Cathy Plourde

2. Actor name and character list
3. Local support lines and resources
4. Names and info supplied from panelists
5. Thank yous, including sponsors

___ Arrange for lighting or sound technicians to meet with actor at least 45 minutes ahead of performance and to be on hand for the performance.

___ Arrange for hands-free mic for the actor, mics for the panel, and mics for roving in the audience.

___ Arrange for set pieces to be on stage:

1. 2 armless chairs
2. A tall stool (without back, or sub 1 additional chair)
3. One 4'-6' table (rectangle)
4. Minimum 15' x 20' performing space

___ Confirm that moderator and any facilitators have all necessary materials,

___ Ready any payments, such as actor fee or honoraria for panelists or their agencies.

LAST MINUTE PRE-SHOW CONCERNS

___ Playbills ready for distributing to audience?

___ Adequate seating, mics, and water for the panelists?

___ Are these items clear of the actor's playing space but easily accessible for a quick transition after the performance?

___ Are people assigned to discreetly monitor the doors? This will help minimize disruption if there are late-comers, and help identify audience members who may be in need of support.

___ Are traditional "trouble" spots (e.g., back and corners of the room) supervised by adults? Disturbances are distracting to the actor, and can be distressing to the audience.

___ Prior to introducing the program, notify the actor when you are about to introduce the play. He will need to be able to hear the introduction to know when to begin.

___ Communicate with the actor regarding the end of the show and how the transition to the post-show will be managed.

PRODUCTION GUIDE

Thank you for choosing to bring *You the Man* to your community. The Production Guide covers the four basic steps to hostiing this play.

STEP 1. PRODUCTION TEAM

STEP 2. PREPARATION
- Preparing Leadership
- Preparing Faculty and Staff
- Preparing Students
- Choosing a Moderator
- Organizing a Panel

STEP 3. PROMOTION

STEP 4. PERFORMANCE & POST SHOW
- Discussion Format Options
- Sample Discussion Approach
- In the Days After *You the Man*
- Moderator Script
- Tips for Moderator and Panelists
- *You the Man* Plot Summary

STEP 1. PRODUCTION TEAM

It's a fair assumption that if you are planning a production of *You the Man*, you are doing so because you see it as a way to address an issue that is alive in your community. Theatre for community engagement on social issues has a different agenda from entertainment, and is rarely something that is ticketed. There are a number of things to keep in mind that will help your success.

- Identify a dedicated site coordinator who can oversee the entire process, including logistics, outreach, and delegating.
- Find a moderator for the performance.
- Secure professional panel members to participate in a post-show discussion.
- If the actor is participating in mounting the production, it's advised that he work with friends or supporters to share in the logistics in planning a performance in a community.

Be sure to have both a site cordinator and a moderator. Two heads make the whole process run much more smoothly, which is of great help to the actor as well as the audience.

Consider what is the best timing for your community. It is not advisable to present the program during testing or exam weeks, special events or spirit weeks, Fridays, or the day before vacation. If the community is stressed by a current event such as a death or other trauma, consider rescheduling.

STEP 2. PREPARATION

The make-up of your intended audience will inform how much and what kind of preparation is required. What follows reflects years of experience presenting *You the Man* in educational settings. The basic tenants can be applied as appropriate for your community.

PREPARING LEADERSHIP

It's critical that the administration and leadership in your community understand that unhealthy relationships, dating violence, and sexual assault can actually mean life and death. You may need to provide reassurances that will help an administrator be confident in approving a performance of *You the Man*.

PREPARING FACULTY AND STAFF

- Share handouts with faculty and staff, such as those by the National Coalition Against Domestic Violence or National Sexual Violence Resource Center, available on their websites.
- Model with faculty and staff how to talk about unhealthy relationships, dating violence, and sexual assault in a non-judgmental way.
- Highlight the fact that DV/SA affects everyone in the community, of all genders, ages, and demographics.
- Coordinate with any curriculum or programming (e.g., orientation, health and wellness, sports, psychology…).

Everyone has a story. Make information about agencies and support services available to faculty and staff as well as students.

PREPARING STUDENTS

You the Man is meant to prompt serious discussion and action toward change while being sensitive to the circumstances of audience members.

- Inform students about the presentation in advance. This is respectful to those who may be dealing with current or past dating or sexual violence.
- Acknowledge the fact that all people, regardless of age, orientation, gender, or class, can be subjected to abuse and violence.
- Emphasize the seriousness of dating violence and sexual violence. Most people do not understand the prevalence of these issues.
- Ridicule or heckling could have a serious negative impact on someone who is involved in dating violence or has experienced sexual abuse.
- Alert all to the fact that supportive professionals will be participating in the program.

If a student requests permission to not attend, honor that request, and take this as an opportunity to open lines of communication with the student.

CHOOSING A MODERATOR

Choose someone to moderate the program who has the respect of the community and who will be comfortable facilitating a discussion between the audience and the panel members. Having someone whose only duty is to moderate the post-show frees the site coordinator to manage the rest of the program.

ORGANIZING A PANEL

Panelists from your local professional community may be willing to volunteer their time, especially as this kind of outreach may be the mission of their agency. In some instances, their organization would willing to make a financial contribution toward the play in return for credit as a sponsor. Conversely, they may require a fee for their time. Either way it is good to establish expectations ahead of time.

Please remember, in licensing You the Man *it is contractual that the program include panel members representing both local domestic violence and sexual assault prevention agencies.*

Two or three panelists are optimal (beyond the actor and moderator). A bigger panel is not better. A large panel only serves to give the community/audience less of a chance to talk. A work-around for involving many people with different kinds of expertise could be to ask them to be in attendance but remain seated in the audience. The moderator can call them out and draw on their support as appropriate.

In most cases the actor can join your panel, but as an addition and not a replacement for local resources. Although he is generally not a mental health specialist, he may be useful or informative to your discussion. The audience has developed a bond with him and they may feel more comfortable in asking him a question. He can pass on anything better handled by an expert.

Consider:

- Dating violence (DV) and Sexual Assault (SA) Advocates
- School nurse, guidance counselor, or social worker
- Coach or law enforcement who is sensitive to the issue

Provide panel members with the **Tips For the Moderator and Panelists** and *You the Man* **Plot Summary** prior to their arrival, and brief them on the post-show discussion strategy.

A script is also advised for the moderator (see sample, p. 80).

Some the most moving moments occur near the end of the discussion. It is not unusual for a person or their family member who has gotten help to find the courage to share their response to the play and speak about how violence has affected them personally.

STEP 3. PROMOTION

There are many in your community who might benefit from attending a performance of *You the Man*. Posters, press releases, video links, and promotional materials can help you communicate with all of your intended audience and guests. Consider different strategies to magnify your efforts:

- Invite parents and caregivers.
- Ask PTAs, school board, booster clubs, or other community groups to attend or send representatives.
- Invite area therapists, DV/SA advocates, and other health professionals.
- Coaches, youth-leadership advisors, or mentors can spread the word through their networks.
- Area nurses, counselors, or administrators from other schools may be interested in previewing the program.
- A trusted journalist could feature the event in local media.
- Press releases accompanied by photos are more likely to be printed.
- Link to information in a social media campaign.
- Ask area hospitals, health centers, and counselors to sponsor or to co-promote the performance.
- Provide tabling opportunities for community programs.
- Offer CEUs to professionals.
- Prepare a playbill for the audience members, to include area agency and help line information, information on the panelists, and any thanks to sponsors as well as the traditional name of the play, author, actor, and list of characters.

Trained advocates who work with survivors and their friends, family, or other supporters are critical to the success of presenting **You the Man** *to your community.*

STEP 4. PERFORMANCE & POST SHOW

Add Verb requires that each performance be followed by a minimum 30-minute talkback period that includes local professional resources. *You the Man* will raise awareness, concern and dialogue, but it cannot provide answers or offer treatment and medical or emotional support.

Presenting **You the Man** *signals to the community that you are willing and open to addressing dating violence, sexual violence, and other sensitive or difficult topics.*

DISCUSSION FORMAT OPTIONS

There are advantages and drawbacks to both whole group and small group discussion formats. Design a post-performance experience that will work best for your community:

- Follow *You the Man* with a whole-group and panel discussion.
- Follow a whole-group and panel discussion with small group follow-ups (e.g., clubs, teams, advisors, or homerooms).
- Follow a whole-group discussion with an invitation to those audience members who wish to talk further with the panalists in designated rooms. This can help honor the time limitations and still provide extra support for those who need it.

People often ask what is the biggest size audience for a performance. It depends on both the venue itself and on what resources you have to run your post-show process.

SMALL GROUP DISCUSSION

Please provide small group facilitators training to be sure they are comfortable and knowledgeable. Share the play's summary, and model how to address common questions and observations with a reminder about any mandated reporting regulations, as appropriate.

LARGE GROUP PANEL DISCUSSION

One of the biggest challenges of a large group discussion is balancing panel members' talking with audience participation. It can be easy for the panelists take over the conversation, but audience participation enriches the program greatly. Methods of fostering audience participation include:

- Use anonymous texting programs or other participator technology.
- Provide note cards in the playbill, or pass out note cards after the performance, asking audience members to write questions. Runners can collect cards during the talk-back, and an appointed person such as the site coordinator or student leader can organize and vet questions before handing them to the moderator.
- Utilize one or two wireless microphones and roving helpers.
- Place a microphone stand in the aisle and invite people to line up for questions.
- Position a spotter to help find raised hands to call upon for questions.
- If there are a number of hands up, it can be more efficient to identify the next couple of people you will call upon.
- Plant an audience member or two with a provokative or plausible question to break the ice.

It undermines all the work you've done when a panelist or audience comment can't be heard.

SAMPLE DISCUSSION APPROACH

1. Start with what the audience has just experienced. This will give a sense of where they are, emotionally, and will encourage participation. For example:
   - *What surprised you in this play? Why?*
   - *Was this realistic? How so or how not so?*
   - *What do you think of differently after seeing this performance?*

2. Ask the audience to share what they already know about abuse and sexual violence. For example:
   - *What are the different types of abuse?*
   - *What are possible signs of abuse that you know of?*
   - *What does it mean to be in a healthy relationship?*

Audiences are drawn in to the seriousness of the issue when they hear about some of the ways people are emotionally controlled by a dating partner. Many recognize this behavior as common; others may have never considered this.

3. Questions to set violence in a larger context could include:
   - *What are the ways people show love or affection, and what are ways people exert control over others?*
   - *Why can behavior from a dating partner be okay at some times and not okay at other times?*

For example: Being met after each class or after work is charming and perhaps a sign of love and affection. Frequent texting or long phone conversations deep into the night are ways people get to know each other. And, yet, at some point any of these things might not be welcomed anymore or the person would just like a little more freedom.

Agreement to engage in sexual activity one or more times is *not* permission for each and every time in the future.

- *How are social expectations seen, and how are they different, for different genders?*
- *How do those expectations impact people's lives?*
- *What does "consent" mean? How do you know if things are consensual, or if they aren't?*

4. For the people in the audience who say, "What can I do to help my friend? What if my friend is aware, but it's still a problem?"

For teenagers and some young adults, their peer world is everything: adults can forget how devastating rifts in friendships and relationships can be. Over and over audience members share how hard it is to have a friend who is struggling, and how awful it can be to say something. Friends and family members may need to get support for themselves. Ask the audience how they might handle these challenges:

- *What are your ideas of how to support a friend who is in an abusive relationship?*
- *What can you do to help a friend who is wondering if what happened was rape?*
- *What things help people to deal with their situation, and might even be harmful?*

5. Closing the discussion:

It is vital that every audience member understand that support is available to them even though the program today has concluded. Direct people to the playbill or other specific places to go for more information in the future.

IN THE DAYS AFTER **YOU THE MAN**

Thank you. You have provided your community with an opportunity and tools to carry the conversation forward. It may help those who have struggled with secrecy and shame to speak with friends and adults. You can be sure that someone desperately needed this play to happen. Time spent on this issue sends a message to those who have been silent that the community is willing to acknowledge their need. Thank you for making a difference.

MODERATOR SCRIPT

INTRODUCING YOU THE MAN

Please turn off cell phones, alarms, and pagers at this time.

> *(Demonstrate with your own device!)*

Today's presentation, *You the Man*, is about unhealthy relationships, dating violence, and sexual assault, which are prevalent in every community across the country. People who have experienced violence often suffer alone and do not know where to turn for help.

We've brought this play to our community today in an effort to open conversation. Violence and abuse deeply impact each of us, directly or indirectly. It may be ourselves or it may be someone we know and care about. This perfornance is a step toward each of us being able to recognize when someone needs support, and how we can best offer that support.

As noted in your program, *You the Man* is performed by one actor playing multiple roles. It is 30 minutes long and will be immediately followed by a discussion. During this time students will be able to ask questions of professionals who are on the panel.

> *(Detail briefly what this will look like.)*

Thank you for your being here today, and now let's begin: *You the Man*, written by Cathy Plourde, directed by _____, and performed for you today by _____.

AFTER THE PERFORMANCE

Thank you for being so attentive. We'll begin the post-show discussion as soon as the panel has assembled. Please use this time to consider your own thoughts and feelings about the play.

After the panel has had a chance to share their personal response to the performance, here is how you can ask your questions:

> *(Provide a description of how questions will be shared with the panel.)*
>
> *(Once panelists are in place:)*

First, thank you for being a part of our conversation today. We'll end at _____, and save ____ minutes for final thoughts.

> *(Thank any sponsors, briefly!)*

To start off the conversation, would you each briefly introduce yourself? Please tell us your name and share something about the performance that struck a note with you.

The site coordinator and designees can be alert to audio and audibility issues, pass mics around for the audience questions, vet written questions for the moderator, and help keep the moderator from running over time.

TIPS FOR MODERATOR AND PANELISTS

*[Site Coordinator:
Please distribute copies in advance and have copies on the day.]*

Dear Moderator and Panelists:

Thank you for taking time to help our community improve our response to violence by participating in the talkback for *You the Man*. The goal of a post-show discussion is to energize our community and open a conversation. The following guides you in your role as a panelist. It has been Add Verb's contractual policy that both domestic violence and sexual assault agency advocates are present for performances of *You the Man*.

- Expect audiences will need a few minutes to transition and warm to a discussion.
- Keep your initial introduction very brief. Sharing a short personal response to the performance will help break the ice. Your credentials and other relevant information can be easily shared in the context of answering a question.
- Provide contact information for you and your organization ahead of time to be included in a playbill.
- Audibility is consistently the biggest complaint from audiences. Please use the available microphones.
- If the moderator hasn't done so, repeat or rephrase the question to be certain you are clear and to make sure the whole audience has heard it. This courtesy reduces audience restlessness.
- Avoid asking yes/no questions of the audience.

- For safety, do not ask the audience to identify if they know someone who has been in an abusive relationship or has experienced sexual violence.
- Asking the audience an honest question, or one with different possible answers, can be an engaging strategy to discover what is important to them.
- Be aware of gender balance in audience participation, and on the panel.
- Please stay succinct and evaluate whether enough has already said on a topic.
- Keep answers jargon-free in an age-appropriate language, without being condescending. This may seem obvious but it's a skill!
- While it may feel rude to interrupt if someone on the panel or in the audience is dominating the conversation, the moderator may need to manage the time and pace of the discussion.
- Avoid responding to overly personal questions from audience members.
- "I don't know" is a legitimate answer.

You may feel compelled to share as much as you can about what you know. Instead, consider this as an opportunity to let people know that you are a resource, and invite people to have further conversation with you later.

YOU THE MAN *PLOT SUMMARY*

[Site Coordinator: please provide to moderator and panelists.]

You the Man *is a 30-minute one-man play. Great care has been taken with the script to give accurate information in a way that does not blame but instead illustrates the seriousness of unhealthy relationships, dating abuse, and sexual violence. This program promotes early intervention, especially by family and friends. What follows is an overview of the story and action in* You the Man *by character. Please note that none of these characters are perpetrators.*

STAN THE MAN. Hip-hop merchant of cool, "here to steer you clear." Stan the Man responds to letters with questions and requests for advice in spoken-word style rhyme. He emphasizes empathy, but also challenges us to become an active bystander. Stan's mother was abused by his father. His teaching points are: gifts or meals for a date does not merit sexual attention; issues of consent; and being intoxicated or high means inability to give consent; and seek support from experts or authorities.

THE VIRGIN LARRY. Virg focuses on cultural pressure to be sexually active. He and his basketball team watch a video created by another player who has violated a girl. When the girl finds out about the video after the fact, she reports it to the police; the team faces expulsion and loss of scholarships. Virg realizes that he is a not-so-innocent bystander who has failed to take action. His teaching points are: pressure for sexual prowess is inappropriately equated with heterosexual manhood; doing or saying nothing is complicity and signals you are siding with the abuser; deferring responsibility and accountability may come with a high price.

MITCHELL. All-around guy who is accepted in most circles. His friend Jana is in increasing danger and he doesn't know how to help her. We watch him first contemplate whether or not to intervene, and then understand that he needs more information from Jana as well as some expert advice himself. He recognizes Jana's safety is at stake, and that he must proceed with caution. His teaching points include: warning signs of abusive behaviors; appropriate and inappropriate strategies for intervention; awareness of and provision for a victim's safety; and victims have the most knowledge about their own situation.

MICHAEL, JANA'S DAD. Dad loves his daughter, yet has trouble articulating his support and concern. No longer as close with Jana as when she was a little girl, he's just admitting his daughter "may" be sexually active, when really, that's old news and she is currently in an abusive relationship. He feels rage, guilt, and helplessness. His teaching points include cultural contradictions within masculinity and fatherhood; communication is not always easy to do well; he needs the help of the community to keep his daughter safe.

DR. WING. He can be read as as either a high school science teacher or a college instructor. He is concerned about the safety of his student, Jana. His personal past with a dating partner spurs him to action when he witnesses controlling behaviors by Jana's boyfriend John. He demonstrates a safe intervention that doesn't alter Jana's schedule. He is prepared with a cover story in case John comes in the room.

OFFICER FRIENDLY. An easy-going speaker who addresses the audience with rhetorical questions, statistics, and the finer points of the law with a charming and humorous affect. His main teaching points are: most sexual assault survivors know their perpetrator; rape or other forced sexual contact may happen with couples who are married or dating; no one is ever asking to be raped; the number of falsely reported rapes are statistically the same as other falsely reported crimes; that most rapes go unreported; and, it is quite possible that a person who violates someone may violate others.

YOU THE MAN IN CULTURAL TRANSLATION: AUSTRALIA

ANN: October 2012 found me in San Francisco for the American Public Health Association conference. Besides spending time in one of my favorite cities, the theme for the conference was 'Prevention and wellness across the lifespan' and I was particularly interested in catching up with the latest research and practice around violence prevention. Back home in Victoria, Australia, the Department of Justice was involved in funding different regional programmes of primary prevention work and I was involved as advisor or evaluator to a number of these. Discussions focused on the provision of capacity building and training, particularly bystander training and the use of champions. Common to all those discussions was recognition of the difficulty of getting men involved, the problem of engaging men in wanting to do this work.

Listening to Cathy present on *You the Man* and the evaluation data, and especially hearing her read just two short excerpts from the script, left me thinking—'wow, we have nothing like this in Victoria' and then, 'so, could we use this?' I rushed up to Cathy after the presentation to ask, did she have any collaborators in Australia, she didn't, would she like to collaborate with Australians, she would, and the idea of a collaboration was swiftly born. Cathy's only stipulation was that in any visit to Australia, there must be kangaroos—I was pretty confident I could deliver on that.

Back home, I examined the state of research funds under my control, and discovered that I did have sufficient un-earmarked funds to start the work off in Australia. Skype conversations got going with a view to Cathy visiting Victoria and us running a program of consultation events around the state with people working in the sector to present the idea of the program and get feedback on the idea. I'd also found collaborators in the form of creative writers Virginia Murray and Patrick van der Werf from the Faculty of Arts at Deakin to help develop the Australian script and started the business of locating a theatre director to work with us.

So, late May 2013 saw Cathy arrive in Victoria and the two of us embark on a road trip around the state for consultation events interspersed with fairly intensive workshop to nut out an Australian script. Fortunately Cathy and I share a liking of food, wine and sightseeing, and there were kangaroos, so the trip went well! The consultations went extremely well, too, with people very enthusiastic about an Australian translation of the program. The consultations confirmed that what was required was a translation of the play for the Australian cultural context rather than any extensive reworking of the play's storylines. By the end of the trip we had a working version of the script to go out to be tested in readings and an enthusiastic mailing list of some 250 plus people in health, education and local government sectors who were interested in being involved.

A series of informal readings held with a range of experts in the field of violence prevention confirmed the applicability and appropriateness of its contents and allowed us to fine-tune the script. We engaged a highly-experienced Australian director, Suzanne Chaundy, to work with us, and by the end of September she had cast two actors to join the team: Glenn Maynard and John Shearman.

Suzanne rehearsed the actors in October and early November 2013, with involvement from our Australian writers Virginia Murray and Patrick van der Werf as well as individuals from the violence prevention field. As a final stage of the rehearsal process, four preview performances were held in November 2013, two for each actor: one with a school audience and one with an adult audience. The secondary schools were in regional Victoria and the adult audiences were at a regional conference of family services providers and early years' staff in Warrnambool, and at an event held as part of the G21 month of action "Stop Violence

Against Women" in Geelong. Feedback from the previews was extremely positive, and provided some helpful suggestions for fine-tuning.

2014 then saw us run a pilot season of 28 performances across the state, where we collected data on the program's short term impact through pre and post surveys, with the post surveys carried out 4-6 weeks after delivery. We were particularly keen to investigate the program's use with adult audiences as well and in a range of different settings within the pilot season: secondary schools, tertiary education institutions, sports clubs, workplaces and community venues.

You the Man's pilot season was a great success. We were really pleased to find how well the program worked with adult audiences as well as with youth in secondary schools. We've delivered in a wide variety of venues and have been delighted by the response in terms of positive constructive conversations, and by the bravery of some of the questions asked. We soon learned the advantages, in the school and sports club settings, of using various forms of technology (texting, TodaysMeet) to allow audiences to ask questions anonymously.

Since the end of the pilot season, we have offered the program across the state of Victoria. We've trained up a third actor, Chris Asimos, and aim to have two actors available at any one time. I continue to be delighted and excited by the positive reactions of those who see the play, and unsolicited feedback that reaches us. As I write this, in early August 2016, we're planning for a further season in 2016 centred around white ribbon day, and already strong interest for 2017, Hopefully we'll have all three actors on the go then. Four years and still going strong.

Prof. Ann Taket, Deakin University, Melbourne, AUS

CATHY: Prof. Ann Taket has produced Australian versions of both *The Thin Line* and *You the Man*. My involvement with the cultural translation of *The Thin Line* was limited but my work on *You the Man* was extensive—and really fun. While there are obvious places that the creative team of producers, director, writers, and actors "Aussified" the script, the language is still remarkably similar to the US version. Most of the changes are in the colloquial language but some changes required a larger overhaul: "Virgin Larry" was changed to "Virgin Barry" because Larry is not a common name in Australia, and VB is a popular beer. Footy (Australian rules football) is the closest equivalent to the US basketball's popularity, crossing all sectors of Australian culture. We had to find comparable stakes to a basketball player's loss of a scholarship within the structure and culture of the football clubs.

The name "Dr. Wing" had the potential of triggering an unwanted racial element in the script, so the writing team chose a simple and unchallenging name which makes the same tone of jokiness as in the US script: "Dr. Wing" was changed to "Dr. Lay". It was a satisfying challenge to work with the writing team to consider each objective, in a line or a stage direction, and decide what could stay and what needed a cultural equivalent.

Traveling across Victoria, Ann and I presented examples of how the US program worked and she very organically engaged a cross-section of organizations at the groundlevel, respectfully looking at how the play migh serve or enhance existing programs in Australia. Because of these measures, the Australian program was effective in both workplace settings and in sporting clubs, as well as schools and trainings.

CP

You the Man
by Cathy Plourde
Australian script adapted by Ann Taket, Virginia Murray, and Patrick Van Der Werf. Directed by Suzanne Chaundy and produced by Prof. Ann Taket (Deakin University, Melbourne, Victoria)

Copyright © CATHY PLOURDE. 2013, 2018.

DO NOT DUPLICATE OR DISTRIBUTE OR PERFORM WITHOUT PERMISSION FROM PLAYWRIGHT
Cathy Plourde holds exclusive right to production. For licensing information or other queries, including permission to quote, contact addverblicensing@gmail.com

A solo performance addressing bystanders, dating abuse, and sexual violence.

By Cathy Plourde

Adapted by Ann Taket, Virginia Murray, and Patrick Van Der Werf

YOU THE MAN AUSTRALIA

Characters:

STAN THE MAN: Merchant of cool with a message.

VIRGIN BARRY: Athlete bumping against the wall of the macho box.

MITCHELL: Bystander compelled to act when his friend Jana is in increasing danger.

MICK: Not a great communicator, struggles to connect with his daughter Jana.

MR. LAY: Academic. Sincere. Models an intervention with his student, Jana.

CONSTABLE FRIEND: Strong and powerful, yet with a sense of humor and doesn't have to push to command respect.

Production notes:

Set: 4 to 6 foot table CSL, the right end of which is angled upstage. Chair behind table with white lab coat on back. Tall stool (no back) down just SR of center line, on same plane as DL corner of table. Chair (no arms) a few feet to the right of stool.

Props: Stan's letters, Mick's phone, Mitch's snack, Dr. Lay's glasses, Virgin Barry's sport-cap water bottle, ball cap and football. On floor behind table, unobtrusively, Mitch's flip chart on easel, facing upstage. Front page or two are always blank. Next page prepped with list and room for writing in one more item, next page prepped with t-chart. Text should be simple block print for maximum readability by audience. Plastic or small bag with other snacks and the marker.

Costume: neutral clothing and footwear, suggested as black t-shirt or button-up and black jeans. Shoes should be low noise makers.

Acting style and lights: with the exceptions of when characters are addressing another character, acting style is direct address to audience. To support this, and support a community dialogue, the lights are on for the stage as well as the house. Mic is hands-free.

1. STAN THE MAN

[Enters from where appropriate to venue, with intention to surprise and take focus. Stan wears sunglasses throughout, except where noted and for effect. Command as though hosting TV program with 'studio audience'. Limited, director approved improv that would acknowledge name of group or town hosting performance before launching into rapidfire opener, e.g. "Can I get me some love?" Or, "What's goin' on Deakin University?" While Stan works DS/front, 'home' is DSC, as if on mark for camera.]

YO! Stan the Man here to steer you clear,

to answer your questions

and provide you with suggestions!

You gotta little lovely?

You getting' cuddly?

You feeling studly?

You come to me, my advice is free!

Stan the Man tells it to you straight up, no set up.

    [Reading.]

Dear Stan The Man, I've a new girlfriend...

    [To "Andy" or the presumed studio camera in audience.]

Hey, congratulations!

    [Reading ahead.]

94 You The Man

Oh, complications…

She's wanting to wait, and I'm wondering how long it'll take — signed, *Andy Ticipation…*

That's a dandy situation, Mr. Andy Ticipation

and I got a good vibration

you gonna get real good at waiting

so savor the flavor of anticipating.

Players, pay attention

and learn something from

this small demonstration for

Mr. Andy Ticipation,

Word 'no':

> *[Striking markedly different girl-pose for each 'no' and comment. Not mocking but these are for a laugh.]*

No, I am not ready.

No, cause you ain't prepared.

Or — Andy, son, the truth might hurt! —

No, not if you were the last man on earth.

Foot off the accelerator, she said no.

So drop me a line, Alligator, and we'll talk about it later.

[Establishes signature signing-out gesture. Steps USC. Swaps sunglasses for cap and football. With back to audience, establishes new character, Virgin Barry, or VB. 'Home' for VB is center left and DS, well off table.]

2. VIRGIN BARRY

[A moment to establish self physically, utilize ball.]

You'd think half the world was getting' it daily. Movies, ads, the net — sex on tap. Easy. But it's not like you can just pick up a ball and get drafted, I don't reckon. They call me the Virgin Barry — VB for short. Great. Is it my fault I'm a kick behind the play? *"Hey VB,"* they say, *"too bad you can't score where it counts."* And if gay-dar is turned on you well it's bums to the wall, mate. I got the first chick I could into bed. How'd it go? Well, no pressure, right? Let's just say I fumbled the ball. Lucky no-one around here keeps score.

[Leaves hat and ball on table, and establishing Mitch as a new character, picks up snack, crosses SR around chair, and directly down DSR to address audience with questions. 'Home' for Mitch for this speech is between DSR and DSC.]

3. MITCHELL

Why do some people think a crap relationship is better than no relationship? Why does someone who is supposed to love someone treat them like crap? Why am I ranting? Okay, here's the situation.

[Pulls up stool, sitting to address audience.]

Eight or ten of us are hanging out and Jana and John are there. I'm more friends with Jana than John, but just friends. Since they started going out, John seems to think that Jana's his property. Anyway. She's hardly said two words this whole time, and then she offered an opinion about something. He jumps all over her. Calls her everything under the sun. *"You're an idiot; you don't know nothin. Why the hell you wearing those tight jeans – they make you look fat"*. And that's for starters.

I'm looking around. Is anybody else gonna say something here? Jana looked like she wanted to curl up and die. I had to say something. *You can't say that, John. Jana, don't put up with this.* Well, John turns on me. "Hey, Mr. Mitchell, she your woman now, or what!?" *No, man. I just don't think…y'know…you should treat her like that.* Couple of others backed me up then. He took that well. He offered to sort me out, then stormed off, dragging Jana with him. If that's how he treats her in public, what else is going on in private? Part of me keeps saying, *not your problem, Mitchell, mind Your Own Business.* But if I just stand there and pretend nothing's wrong, doesn't that make me part of the problem?

    [Referring to snack.]

I'm going to need more of this. You want anything from the shop?

    [Leaves snack on table, trades for Mick's phone. Circles UL of table to DSL.]

4. MICK

[Contemplating phone, then chosing to address his audience. 'Home' is DSL of DSL of table corner.]

All that stuff that we might consider feminine, unbloke-like—well, you need all that to be a good father. *Father.* Jana's called me dada, daddy, dad, then, when her mother and I divorced, "Mick"—that hurt somehow. They grow up so fast. I used to say that when Jana got old enough to y'know…well, there'd be no "y'know!" If I even get to meet any of her friends, I'm lucky. There's a very independent young woman who lives at the other end of this phone.

[Having speed dialed, waits briefly for pickup on other end of line.]

Jana, hi, it's Mick… how are you?… Good, good…. Well, no I just haven't seen much of you lately – you seem to spend most of your free time with John… Uh, I know, um, how are things going with him?

[To audience.]

—Oh no, my little girl isn't old enough to have sex yet, maybe when she's thirty, thirty-five—

[To Jana.]

Why?

[To audience.]

Why…?

[To Jana.]

Becaaaauusssse, because I wanted to know if — if you two — wanted to go to — the footy — or the zoo — sometime.

> *[To audience.]*

Did I really say that?

> *[Turns US, leaving mobile on left end of table, swaps for Lay's glasses. Adopts Mr. Lay physicality and voice as donning lab coat.]*

5. MR. LAY

> *[As finishing putting on coat, crosses DC to address his audience.]*

Okay, class: have you any questions before tomorrow's exam? No, Toni, you won't fail if you spell my name wrong again. L — A — Y. Lay. Ian. Are there questions about the exam…? No? All right then, except for Jana — I need to talk to you about your assignment — Thank you, you can go now. Study hard. Ah, Jana, have a seat and let me find your paper…

> *[While speaking, returns to US of table to mime rifling unseen stack of papers, then crosses USR to establish and close door. Throughout, establish/place Jana on the stool with gesture and directional looks and clearly maintain respectul physical distance.]*

No, no, we ended early today, so we should have a full five minutes before your boyfriend who drops you off and picks you up after class each and every day gets here. Please, sit down for just a moment.

> *[Handing Jana her paper.]*

Here you go. Ah, I didn't really want to talk about your assignment…

Well, yes, in a manner of speaking, something's wrong… this is awkward…

> [Places the SL chair for himself and sits, knees front].

While my job is to teach science, the curriculum and my syllabus aren't more important than the *Homo sapiens* exchanging carbon dioxide for oxygen in front of me…

> [Joke fails on Jana.]

I can't ignore my students when… well…. Do you remember two classes ago you were a few minutes late finishing up a lab—no, don't apologize. However, I observed that your boyfriend John was very unhappy with having to wait for you and then—no—no, Jana, no, that was not your fault.

> [Her response is enough to motivate cross DSL.]

You did not MAKE him get upset. John chose to get upset. This was not a question of you being at fault, this was a case of—of…

Jana, I saw John grab you by the elbow, here, and twist. The words he used as he removed you from this classroom were not kind. Last class, I noticed you had bruises—no, no, you're right—

> [Without being threatening, makes quick cross USR to prevent her from leaving just yet.]

You don't want to talk to your teacher about your personal life. That's precisely why I had waited until today to approach you… You know the student bulletin board near the lift? There's a poster there for a local agency. It has a phone number on the bottom. Or, online you can find several help line numbers. I'm worried about you, Jana, and—

> [Snap over right shoulder to door.]

—Ah! Hello, John! I see you're right on time to pick up Jana! If only my students were as punctual. No, please, come in—this isn't a private conversation. Jana will be right with you.

> [Returning attention to Jana, studiously casual.]

So, as I was saying… I'm worried about your paper. If, as I suggest, you submit it for the faculty prize—and I really think you've explained the moral complexity of stem cell research with great clarity—you'll need to check the submission guidelines. Please call that number for more information.

> [Dismissing them, cross US to return lab coat to chair.]

Now, if you two will excuse me. I hope you both have a pleasant day.

> [Leaves glasses, shift to Stan, sunglasses and stack of letters. Cross DSC to address his audience.]

6. STAN THE MAN

> [From his mark. The seriousness of the letters help define pace.]

We're back with a stack. It's time to find what's on your mind!

    [Reads.]

Dear Stan The Man, if I buy a girl dinner, I wanna go home a winner. Any advice?

Listen up, I'm not saying it twice.

Mr. Un-Happy Meal, here's how I feel:

Dinner's a date not a deal!

It's not too late—just get real.

    [Reads. When he figures out he's been punked, he wryly thinks it's funny.]

Stan the Man, I could use some help around this place, when you gonna call your poor old neglected mothe—Oh! Look, Ma, I'm busy—who let this through? I'll call you this weekend, I promise. Next letter!

    [Reads.]

Dear Stan the Man, a friend of mine is in a violent relationship. He's afraid to get help, and he's afraid to leave. How do you help a friend who is gay and not out, get out of danger?

Heterosexual, bisexual, transgender,

gay, lesbian, questioning,

it's a situation wanting liberation, adjusting.

Safety first, get him through the worst

one step at a time—my advice—call the local help line.

He needs a personalized plan, not just Stan the Man. Good luck, all right?

    [Reads.]

Stan the Man—I thought it was true love forever, but we broke up, and I'm being tagged in some embarrassing photos online—and people have written some ugly things. And still worse, my ex's friends are making it personal, filling up my in-box with hate mail.

Today this beau, this photo—

"yeah, that's cool"

but tomorrow maybe you wanna apply the gag rule 'cause someone's become a real tool.

How can a smile so sweet—flip the switch—be the creep you can't delete?

Virtual friends, virtually impossible to undo—

like a tattoo you wish you could re-do,

maybe even take back the "I love you?"

Sorry for the hassle, but we all gotta recall—

Facebook's not private your-space—it's a public chase.

Catch yourself a predator, get a stalker's disrespect:

it's technology feeding ugly pathology, electronic punches with no apology—hey, I'm sorry.

Remove the tags, maybe take down your site;

re-think photographing how you spend your night.

Threats and defamation? Take it to the police station.

> *[Turns back USC, drop glasses and letters. Quick step to Mitch's flipchart, bag with snacks, and marker.]*

7. MITCHELL

> *[Places flip chart on SL end of table, if table is big enough. Otherwise, easel can have legs extended and chart can tuck to left edge of table.]*

Okay. Welcome to the think tank. I've got protein bars here for those who think it'll help. Now. A friend of mine, Jana, is in an abusive and increasingly dangerous relationship. Yeah? No? Last night John put his fist through a wall at a party, about an inch to the right of Jana's head. It's time to fly the flag here. So—what are my options?

> *[Flips paper over on chart to reveal list.]*

This is what I've got so far… *Mitch talk to John.* Not open to friendly constructive criticism, and definitely not from me. *Beat up John.* Sure.

> *[An implied 'no'.]*

I don't want to risk making things worse for Jana. *Talk to Jana's friends etc.* Get this—one of Jana's friends said she thought she'd persuaded Jana to dump him. Great. Well. The next day… Jana went right back to him. The friendship went a bit sour after that.

Call help line. But "help line"…? It makes it sound like life and death.

> *[Truth of this is evident, scary; he moves on.]*

Rescue Jana. Sure. Chivalry. Just get on a white horse. And then what? She may not want to be rescued. And, he punched a hole in the wall because she wanted to leave a party. What's he going to do when she wants to leave him? So what are my options?

> *[Scribbling out rescue, talk, beat up, then referring to what's left.]*

No. No. No. I can ask around — see what other people know, get the full picture. I'll call that number. Or, better yet, I'll make Jana call. Listen to me — just someone else trying to push her around. I don't even know what she wants to do. RIGHT.

> *[Writes in.]*

Talk… to… Jana.

> *[Leave marker on table. Transition to Constable Friend. Circle behind stools and USR chair to enter and address audience from DSR. 'Home' is DSR to DSC].*

8. CONSTABLE FRIEND

Did you know that approximately 73% of all rapes are committed by perpetrators known to the victim? A friend, family member, acquaintance, colleague…? That's a barbeque stopper all right. My name is Constable Friend. That's right, Friend by name, not necessarily by nature…

Now, in every audience there's always someone who has a story. The same story. *Excuse me, sir, but I know a guy whose life was ruined when he was falsely accused of rape by a woman wanting to get revenge.* To which I reply: there's no statistical difference between falsely reported rapes and falsely reported crimes in general. True. More often, rapes go unreported. Also true. Why would a rape go unreported, you ask? Good question. Remember that 73%? Friends, family, acquaintances. As for that other thing people always say, no, she didn't 'ask for it.' No one is ever asking to be raped, and blaming the victim isn't very helpful. As for falsely claiming rape to get some sort of revenge, weeeellll, I wouldn't recommend trying it.

[Turns and steps to get ball cap and ball, now as VB.]

9. VIRGIN BARRY

Sex and drugs and alcohol—you gotta talk it up. It's all about the game—how many chicks you can score before full time. So far this season, VB's on fire—burstin' outta the pack, goin' hard, headin' for goal, straight through the middle. You see where I'm going with this. I'm doing media training for the inevitable post match interviews.

Then there's my best mate, Tom. Tommo the Terminator. A real beast on the field. Team leader on and off. He got in some trouble—a girl was saying he raped her. I asked him straight out, man to man. Boy was he mortified. I felt like a real prick. Hey, if he says he didn't do it, well I believe him. The girl was sorry she ever brought it up. But then a few weeks later, Tommo says to the team he's got a home movie… A little way into watching it, it's clear that this girl doesn't have any idea she's on funniest home videos. And she wasn't all that willing either. She said 'stop' a few times, but the Terminator was renowned for being unstoppable once he crossed the white line. It was…bad. Not just the video either. *Tommo, you're a legend,* they were shoutin,' *you're a sick bastard—you the man, ha ha.* What was wrong with these people? And I wonder about that girl from before, and if I was just believing who I wanted to believe.

> *[Turns back to table, swap cap and ball for snack. Repeats Mitch's cross, behind stool and chair, to DSR.]*

10. MITCHELL

> *[Catching audience observing him.]*

All right. Now I'm just eating because I'm nervous.

> *[Gets rid of snack.]*

Jana does her studying at the library while John's at work. I decide to talk to her there. He won't be around.

> *[He sees and approaches, DSR. Dialogue fluctuates: Jana's voice, noted in italicized quotes; Mitch to Jana, noted in italics; and to audience.]*

*Jana. Hi. Hey, I'm glad I found you! I, uh, I—*I don't know what I'm doing—*I just jump in—I'd like to talk to you for a minute because, uh, see, I'm worried about—*She cuts me off. "*Sorry but I'm studying here. That table's free*". Okay…

> *[Sits down, SL chair.]*

Bit later, she walks past, and drops a note next to me.

> *[He picks it up and reads.]*

"Meet me in the 007 stack in three minutes, but don't let anyone see you." 007?

> *[Action of checking time, finding the stacks, waiting for her DSR.]*

Jana, hey, which Bond movie is this? She says John's friends report to him who she talks to, *"because he's jealous of other guys"*. This is abusive. She says, *"John's not abusive. He loves me. He'd never hit me"*. This is abusive behavior — controlling who you talk to. *Jana, even if he hasn't hit you, this controlling crap, putting you down in front of people – no one can see those marks. And hey, what about that hole in the wall, how close was that to your head?* She looked startled at first, but then she says I don't know him like she does. So?? *I'm sure he's got his good points, Jana, I mean you wouldn't go out with a guy who – ah, it's just –* She says she has to go now. *Jana, if you ever need someone to listen, I'm always here in 007.* She doesn't laugh, she just says: *"Please don't make it worse"*. And she goes. Great. So she knows it can get worse. Great.

> *[Has ended DSC. Turn US for Stan's glasses and next letter.]*

11. STAN THE MAN

> *[Takes mark, reads.]*

Dear Stan The Man, what if a guy and a girl are both drinking, and they have sex? Later she says she hadn't wanted to, but was too messed up to be able to say stop. I say that she was drinking and shouldn't have been drunk if she didn't want to fool around, but my friend Joe says that's rape. Thanks for steering us clear.

No problem, that's why I'm here.

Your man Joe knows which way the wind blows, what the rules are.

The "we-were-both-drinking" thinking — that's a trap not gettin' you far.

You drunk driving, it's a matter-o-fact

it's who's driving the car sits behind the bars,

not your friend passed out inside you took for a ride.

> *[He starts to leave but can't let go of the issue.]*

It's a tragedy if you ain't capable of sympathy, don't know empathy,

can't imagine bein' in someone else's skin. It's time you step in.

Imagine this, imagine your sister, your mother, one good friend or another.

Maybe you on the telephone, maybe you both alone…

Okay, now, she's says she's got something important to say.

She's seeing shades of grey, so she needs you to listen and not go away.

You hear her fear, and she's got your ear.

She's gotta friend, charming and smart who's been after her heart.

She tells you something bad happened, she thinks, that maybe she had had a little too much to drink —

or maybe she had nothing to drink —

and she tells you they were getting a little friendly —

cut to where she's saying no.

She pushes his hand away. He tries again anyway.

She says no, number two. He tries again, now what's he gonna do?

And this time as he's crossin' the line,

she stays really quiet and still

and he thinks he's gotta green light to cruise down this hill.

He's not slowin', he keeps goin' —

She's already said no-no-no,

but all that's in his head is go-go-go.

Doctor's analysis, she's got paralysis,

she can only watch it, she can't stop it.

This is making war, not love.

I can't tell you more.

G is for "green," G is for "go," but the G is silent in "that's enough."

This is your sister. Or your friend. And yeah, I'll end.

Removing illusions, avoiding confusions.

Empathy, like sympathy, only better.

Stan the Man. Thanks for the letter.

> *[Cross to leave glasses USR corner of table, stepping to get phone, completing cross DSL.]*

12. MICK

> *[On phone wth Jana's mother.]*

Jana hasn't said anything to you either? Look—I understand you're upset—Can we just focus on Jana? I'll call you as soon as I talk to her. Bye—[*beat*] I know. Me too.

> *[Having hung up, to his audience.]*

Her mother and I hardly ever see her, so how could we know? Jana's friend tells me what's going on. It's my job to take care of her. What I don't understand is how this has happened. I've let her down. I didn't realize it could hurt so much. She's got to get out of this.

> *[Having speed dialed.]*

Jana, it's Mick—it's your father. Is this a good time? We need to talk.

> *[Ending near stool, ear to phone and tight turn from audience. Leaves phone. Assumes Constable Friend, repeating cross circling stool arriving DSR, using home area.]*

13. CONSTABLE FRIEND

If a person's been raped, they'd know it, right? Not always. What if there was alcohol or drug use involved? What if they'd been raped by someone they've previously been intimate with? Frankly, there's no mention in the law of the right to have sex with someone who is unwilling. Even if they are married or dating.

You know, people always want to know why I do this — why I willingly get up and talk about such cheerful matters as sexual assault? Maybe one of those sexual assault victims was my sister, so it's become my mission to spread the word. Or maybe there's a young transgender person here whose life is made hell by some local toughs, and I'm the voice of tolerance coming to the rescue. Or, it could be that Crimestoppers was tipped off about a certain someone who's been dropping date-rape drugs at parties. Now any of that, or none of that, could be why I do this. But not one of us, myself included, has to wait for the excuse of something terrible happening before we act like we care.

> *[Turns and steps to table for ball and cap. Assumes VB.]*

14. THE VIRGIN BARRY

So, football — the great metaphor for life itself. Boundaries, rules. Most guys are maybe waiting for the ump to blow the whistle. What do we do when there's no whistle?

> *[Implied 'keep going' or 'got away with it'.]*

But hey, I wasn't even in the field of play. So we get a call from the league lawyer. The girl in the "funniest video" went to the police. We might all be in the shit, he says, and we can kiss the draft goodbye. The Terminator lives up to his name. But me? I did nothing. Nothing.

[Turns to trade ball and cap for Lay's glasses.]

15. MR. LAY

My first lab partner at uni…mmm…chemistry at first sight. It ended in heartbreak; mine. I finally discovered why she wouldn't, well, couldn't trust me. She had been abused, emotionally and then later physically by her first boyfriend. It would take her years to ever trust again. Violence starts a chain reaction, and what he did to her, in turn, continues to impact and hurt others. And that's why I spoke out to Jana.

[Turns, leaves glasses. Steps to phone to resume last position of phone to ear and back to audience. Turns to face audience, defeated. Sits.]

16. MICK

So. I wanted to say, *I am your father and I would do anything to make you happy. I know I can't live your life for you; that you have to make your own choices. But even if you are all grown up, you're not alone. I will listen. I will always believe you. I will always love you. I will not judge you. I will just listen.*

But what I said instead was—

[Resuming arm position, ear to phone.]

Dammit, Jana, why didn't you tell me?

[Leaves phone, trade for marker.]

17. MITCHELL

I called the local help line. I told them my name was ah Bob…Robertson. She told me right away that this was an anonymous confidential call and I didn't need to worry. We talked through Jana's situation.

[Flip to t-chart page. Stays/Leaves, with under Stays: be abused, loss of self esteem, might lose job, loss of friends/support, could get hurt.]

The list of what happens if she decides to stay is essentially the same as what happens if she leaves. And the bad news is that the time Jana's in the most physical danger…

[Drawing arrows from items from one list to the other side of the t-chart.]

…is when she decides to leave. If Jana calls them, they can help her set up a safety plan. A safety plan? I called the help line because I wanted to get some answers. It was good to hear I'd been doing things right, but there's no quick fix.

[Trade marker for sunglasses, moves to DSC.]

18. STAN THE MAN

You're probably wondering
how I got to be so smart,
why I play this part,
how I got this attitude.
All-right.
I'll give you a clue.

> *[Removes sunglasses.]*

I watched my father beat my mother. And then he would drag her to their bedroom. My mother couldn't leave him, and she couldn't press charges. The cops stopped coming.

> *[Replaces sunglasses.]*

My father is yelling,
my mother is screaming,
then silence,
I'm relieved.
But there's no telling
if my mum was crying
that time
I was conceived.

> *[Leaves glasses on stool. From there, assume Constable Friend, turn to address his audience.]*

19. CONSTABLE FRIEND

If it were your mother or your daughter or your sister or your brother or your friend, you would want justice to the fullest extent of the law. If it's ever you, get yourself the help you need. Do it for yourself. Do it so there's not a next victim.

> *[Having ended DSC, turn for ball and cap. Step off, DS and away from table.]*

20. THE VIRGIN BARRY

So, I did nothing to stop the broadcast, and I didn't even think about leaving, so that means I'm not an innocent bystander. Is that fair on me? But, how fair is it to be raped? If I had stood up and left, maybe others would have followed. Maybe they were looking for a way out, too. Maybe Tommo might think again without his cheer squad.

> *[Turn to leave cap and ball, trade for Lay's glasses]*

21. MR. LAY

I could turn away, just teach my class, but I can't. What if next time John does more than just bruise Jana?

> *[Pick up phone, trade sunglasses. Establish self as Mick, stepping forward DSC, open to audience.]*

22. MICK

I need help keeping my daughter safe. Who will help me? Please.

> *[Turning out, beat before quick step to flip chart. Rip page off and write large "listen".]*

23. MITCHELL

> *[Stepping to side of chart, CS]*

All I can do is speak up when something isn't right. And I can listen to Jana, give support, not judge. Give her time.

> *[Trade marker for sunglasses. DSC.]*

24. STAN THE MAN

In this time
in my words and my rhyme
I've shed some light
on what's wrong and what's right.
It's time for the violence to end,
and it starts with you and your friends.
But Stan the Man can't hold your hand.
You the man—ladies too.
Now. Whatcha you gonna do?

> *[Exit. Return for bow and acknowledgement.]*

www.ingramcontent.com/pod-product-compliance
Lightning Source LLC
Chambersburg PA
CBHW060202050426
42446CB00013B/2947